GANGSTER
SPEAK
A DICTIONARY OF CRIMINAL AND SEXUAL SLANG

GANGSTER SPEAK

SPEAK

A DICTIONARY OF CRIMINAL AND SEXUAL SLANG

JAMES MORTON

GANGSTER SPEAK: A DICTIONARY OF CRIMINAL AND SEXUAL SLANG

This edition first published in 2006 by
Virgin Books Ltd
Thames Wharf Studios
Rainville Road
London
W6 9HA

First published in the UK in 2002 by Virgin Books Ltd

ISBN 0 7535 0699 8

Typeset by Phoenix Photosetting, Chatham, Kent
Printed and bound in Great Britain by
BookMarque Ltd

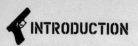# INTRODUCTION

Many years ago, shortly after I had become a solicitor, I went to Hastings to defend a man accused of office breaking. He was completely frank. He would plead guilty. He had, he said, had his children with him. I threw up my hands in horror saying how much longer he would get for this appalling piece of parental behaviour. I was swiftly put in my place. 'Housebreaking instruments, twirls, boys and girls, me children.' It was only one of a number of errors I made in those days. I did not know what 'to go case' was. I was not alone in my ignorance. A colleague of mine thought that being on the river was a potential alibi. A barrister at Horseferry Road Magistrates' Court, hearing the police say that his client had legged it, told the magistrates that the reason the man was late was that he had walked to court. I decided that it would not hurt if I tried to learn the language rather than having to say 'What?' at every second sentence. The distance between users and non-users was exemplified by Judge Peter Mason, a judge of many years' standing, who wrote in *The Magistrate* in December 1988, 'I discovered the other day (though I'm told the phrases have been around for some time) that in certain quarters every prison sentence has its label.' They had probably been around for fifty to a hundred years when the judge penned his article. I decided to learn.

Slang is ephemeral. It changes fast and words come and go and then return to favour after decades. Rhyming slang is particularly subject to change and invention. Slang can also be localised. Glossaries of American prison slang are keen to point out that what is used in Michigan is not necessarily common in Texas. The same applies to American street gangs. The Crips use words which would be anathema to their archenemies the Bloods.

Of course, the real interest is not in knowing that, say, a Black Maria means a police van, but why it is so known. Some words can easily be defined. Others like Black Maria have their origins firmly wedged in folklore. I have tried to provide definitive explanations for many of the words or give alternative suggestions but I doubt that now anyone will be able to say that the derivation of Old Bill is definitely one thing rather than another.

1

GANGSTER SPEAK: A DICTIONARY OF CRIMINAL AND SEXUAL SLANG

Interpreting criminal slang is not an exact science and it is likely that some readers will disagree violently with some of the definitions or will say they have never heard of such usage. One example would be kanga, meaning a prison officer and deriving from the rhyming slang. People in the north of England possibly have not come across what southern criminals think of as everyday usage. They, certainly those from Liverpool, prefer The Germans. If readers have alternative meanings or explanations for the words in this book I will be pleased to hear from them. I have tried to ensure that the words in this small dictionary have been in use within the last half of the twentieth century.

My thanks are due to many but particularly to Razor Smith for his help in compiling entries on current British prison slang. I know he had in mind at one time to compile his own book and he has been extremely generous in passing his research on to me.

When I first wrote *Lowspeak* I received a letter from Paul Beale, the editor of *A Concise Dictionary of Slang*. Could he extract some 180 words for his new edition? Sadly there was not one. However, we continued a correspondence until his death. I was the pupil. There was rarely a word of which he had not heard or of which he could not provide an explanation. I hope this book would have pleased him.

List of abbreviations to be used in this book;		**Jam**	Jamaican
		Jap	Japanese
abb	abbreviation	**NZ**	New Zealand
Aus	Australian	**NYPD**	New York Police Department
Bl	Black		
c	circa	**m/cycle**	motorcycle
Can	Canadian	**orig**	originally
euph	euphemism	**prob**	probably
ex	from	**pl**	plural
Fr	French	**pris**	prison
Glas	Glaswegian	**qv**	quis videt
Hisp	Hispanic	**Russ**	Russian

2

SA	South African	**US**	United States
Scot(s)	Scottish	**WI**	West Indian
UK	United Kingdom		

A

AB: (US) Aryan Brotherhood; a right wing White and biker prison gang.

ABROAD: out and about and up to no good, particularly at night.

ACCELERATOR: (US) an arsonist, ex the fluid used to start a fire.

ACCIDENT, TO HAVE AN: 1. to be arrested, 'I had an accident' = 'I was caught.' 2. to foul oneself (euph), 'I had an accident last night.'

AC/DC: bisexual, ex the electric current.

ACE: 1. very good. 2. (Bl) a good person. 3. one dollar. 4. to kill.

ACE IN THE HOLE: a person or object who or which gives an overwhelming advantage. In stud poker the first card is dealt face down and is known as the hole card. If it is an ace it is of particular value. In the song of the same name by Cole Porter an *Ace in the Hole* may be a girl 'on that old tenderloin' providing money from prostitution, or a loan or present from the 'old folks at home'.

ACE OF SPADES: 1. a widow. 2. a particularly dark-skinned Afro-American. 3. the vagina.

ACID: 1. lysergic acid. 2. (Aus) impertinence. Nicholas Monsarrat, *The Cruel Sea*, 'Don't come the acid with me.'

ACROSS THE PAVEMENT: a wages snatch.

ACTION: a bet placed through a bookmaker.

ACTION, WHERE'S THE?: where is there excitement? E.g. a card game or other form of gambling or a place to meet women, more specifically prostitutes.

ADMINISTRATION: (US) the ruling body of a crime family.

AGAINST THE CLOCK: in a hurry.

AGG(RO), (A SPOT OF); 1. trouble, as in being arrested. 2. annoyance, 'The copper was giving me aggro so I clumped him.'

AGGY; aggravated burglary.

AIR DANCE; death by hanging.

AIRING, TO TAKE SOMEONE FOR AN; to kill.

AIR MAIL; objects thrown through windows at prison guards.

ALADDIN'S CAVE; hideaway for stolen goods, see also slaughter.

ALIAS MAN; a useless criminal or worthless person generally. Originally 18c English, now almost exclusively Black slang.

ALKALI, ALKI; bootleg liquor.

ALKI; a drunk.

ALL DAY; (US) a life sentence.

ALL DAY AND A NIGHT; (US) life without parole.

ALL ON TOP; superficial, specifically applied to police evidence in the form of a weak case.

ALPHONSE; ponce, ex German.

ALPS, TO GO OVER THE; to be sent to Dartmoor Prison.

AMAMI NIGHT; a regular time for a cell search by prison officers, ex a popular advertisement for a hairwash on a Friday in preparation for partying at the weekend.

AMBULANCE CHASER; a lawyer who relies on attending hospitals or funeral homes to obtain clients.

AMERICAN WAY; coexistence between rival organised crime families.

AMICO; a friend or associate of a crime family.

AMICO MIO; my friend, not an inducted member of the Mafia.

AMICO NOSTRO; our friend, an individual inducted into the Mafia.

ANCHOR: 1. a stay of execution in a death penalty case. 2. a bribed juror who will be expected to vote for an acquittal and so cause a disagreement or, in England, where 10–2 majority verdicts are permitted, to try to influence at least two others to vote with him.

ANCHOR, TO SWALLOW THE: 1. to give oneself up to the police. 2. to retire from crime.

ANGEL: 1. someone supplying money to finance a crime (also theatrical). 2. a sandwichboard man. 3. a passive homosexual.

ANGEL DUST: PCP, phencyclidine.

ANGLE: to scheme.

ANGLER: 1. a thief who steals from ground floor windows with a rod or pole. As fewer people leave their windows open and unbarred the art form is dying in Britain. However, the trend is now to take keys from hall tables by fishing through the letterbox. In February 2002 Liverpool footballer John Arne Riise had his BMW X5 stolen after his keys

were taken in this way. See also Polefishing. 2. a pickpocket.

ANIMAL: 1. a person without any moral code, a psychopath. 2. (boxing) an African-American, 'He only has animals in his stable.' 3. strongarm man working for a gambling syndicate.

ANKLE: an illegitimate child.

APACHE INDIAN JOB: a firebomb which leaves nothing.

APPLE CORE: £20, apple core = score.

APPLE, THE: position, apple core = score, 'You know the apple.'

ARCHER: £2,000, ex the amount alleged to have been given by Jeffrey Archer to the prostitute, Monica Coughlan.

ARCTIC EXPLORER: drug addict. The play is on the word snow (qv).

ARM CANDY: a young attractive woman who accompanies an elderly male to expensive restaurants etc. She will usually be expected to provide some form of sexual service.

ARM, ON THE: eating and drinking without payment, usually by a police officer. In return the officer is expected to prevent minor trouble in the café or restaurant and inform the proprietor of any impending raid. It is a matter of continuing debate whether this is the lowest level of police corruption or is indeed an example of good community policing.

ARM, THE: the Buffalo, New York, faction of the Cosa Nostra.

ARM, TO PUT THE A. ON: to ask for a loan.

ARMY: a person, often a tramp, with one arm.

ARSE: 1. the buttocks. Until late 17c the word was Standard English but then became mere slang. 2. a foolish person.

ARSE BANDIT: a predatory homosexual.

ARSE-END: the dregs. 'Lagos is the arse-end of Africa.'

ARSEHOLED: very drunk, poss. ex the diarrhoea which will follow a heavy night's drinking.

ARSEWIPE: a contemptible person.

ASHES: TO HAVE ONE'S A. HAULED: sex, usually with a prostitute or stranger.

ASSASSIN'S SPECIAL: a .22 automatic handgun equipped with a silencer.

AT IT: 1. thieving, either generally or on a specific occasion. 2. having sexual intercourse.

ATTACHÉ CASING: (US) collecting bribes so large they must be carried in a brief case.

AUNTIE: 1. a madam in a brothel. 2. an elderly male homosexual.

AVIATION BLONDE: a woman with dyed blonde hair, ex blonde hair, black box. The black box refers to the flight recorder and box refers to the vagina.

AWAY: to be in prison.

AWAY, TO HAVE IT; 1. to escape after a theft. 2. to have sexual intercourse.

AWAYS; people in a team currently in prison who are supported by those remaining at liberty. Albert Donaghue, *The Krays' Lieutenant.*

AXE; 1. a knife. 2. a razor 3. a guitar.

AXEMAN; a prison barber.

AXE-WOUND; the vagina.

AXLE; a bribe, ex axle grease.

B

BABANIA: (US) heroin and specifically heroin trafficking.

BABBLER: a thief (Aus) babbling brook = crook.

BABBO: a straight person, often a dupe.

BABY FATHER: a pimp, usually Black. Marilyn Wisbey, *Gangster's Moll*, 'We did keep Parker's security camera on loan as we did need it for any baby fathers knocking on the door.'

BABYLON: 1. (WI 20c) police, as in 'Look out, here comes Babylon.' Deriving from the belief amongst Rastafarians that the Biblical Babylon was a place of the utmost evil. In the Mandrake Club trial in the 1970s following an affray in West London, much turned on the use of the word and whether it had been a signal to attack the police. 2. England. 3. White people generally.

BABYSITTER: 1. (Can) prison officer. 2. a bodyguard especially of a witness under police or federal protection.

BACK, AT THE: (US) drugs taken one after another.

BACKDOOR MAN: 1. (US Bl) a sodomite. 2. a married woman's lover who leaves by the back door as the husband comes through the front. Alan Sillitoe, *Saturday Night and Sunday Morning.*

BACK GATE DISCHARGE: (US) 1. the death of a prisoner, taken out of the back gate so as not to upset other inmates. 2. parole.

BACKING AND FILLING: the art of filling the mark (qv) with confidence prior to the trick being worked on him.

BACK SCUTTLE: (Aus) 1. vaginal intercourse from behind. 2. to enter a house the back way.

BACK STOP: 1. (Aus) a person looked to for support, ex cricket, the man behind the wicketkeeper. 2. a man who works directly behind the victim of pickpocketing. Particularly common in Chicago in the 1930s.

BACK STREET BUTCHER; an abortionist, ex the mess often made of the unfortunate client.

BACK UP; 1. (US) to allow the blood to return to the glass during a vein shot. 2. to distend the vein during drug taking. 3. (US) serial sex with a woman. 4. to refuse a connection for fear that the addict may in turn be a stool pigeon. 5. assistance given by a police officer to a colleague.

BACON; (Pris) a child molester, bacon bonce = nonce.

BAD; (US Bl) very good. A reversal of values.

BAD COUNT; a quantity of drugs smaller than that paid for.

BAD FALL; (US) an arrest when the rapper (qv) refuses to withdraw the charge.

BADGE; (US) a police officer.

BADGER; originally a man who stole clothes in a brothel, now a blackmailer.

BADGER GAME; a confidence trick in which a man goes to an hotel with a young woman or one who appears to be very young. When both are partially undressed but before intercourse has taken place the h u s b a n d / f a t h e r / uncle enters the room and demands compensation for the ordeal to which the girl has been put.

BAD RAP; (US) a sentence in excess of 20 years.

BAD SCENE; (US) a situation, particularly in the drug trade, when trouble is likely to break out at any minute.

BAD TRIP; an unpleasant experience whilst taking drugs, particularly LSD.

BAG; 1. the scrotum. (US) 2. a small packet of narcotics. A nickel bag is five dollars and a dime bag one of ten dollars. Green points out that whilst the terms remain the same the quantity and quality provided diminishes. 3. a condom.

4. personal taste as in 'Drugs aren't my bag.'

BAG, IN THE: drunk, ex the practice of liquor stores in supplying alcohol in brown paper bags.

BAG, TO HOLD THE: (Aus) to bear the risk of a criminal enterprise.

BAGGAGE: (US) 1. A watcher at a card game. 2. A woman sent to South America for the purposes of prostitution.

BAGGAGE BOX/BOY: (US) homosexual prostitute offering active as opposed to passive sex to clients.

BAGGED: 1. (UK) arrested. 2. (US) drunk.

BAGGER: a ring snatcher, ex the French *bague*, a ring. Should anyone think this practice is obsolete an instance occurred in a restaurant in Knightsbridge in 2001 when thieves entered and, after threatening the staff, pulled off a woman diner's rings.

BAGMAN: 1. (US) a collector

and deliverer of bribes, often a junior police officer. 2. (Aus) a vagrant. 3. The member of a robbery team whose job it is to collect the cash.

BAG OF SHELLS: (Aus) an unconsidered trifle ex bagatelle.

BAGPIPE: sexual intercourse where the penis is placed in the armpit.

BAIL UP: (Aus) 1. to rob. 2. to hold-up in the sense of stopping for a chat.

BAKED POTATO: goodbye, baked potato = later.

BALANCE, UNE: (Fr) an informer.

BALD TYRE BANDIT: traffic policeman, ex his checking on the roadworthiness of vehicles.

BALE: (US) a pound or half kilo of marijuana.

BALL: 1. (UK to end of 1950s) daily allowance of meat in prison. 2. (US) to have sexual intercourse.

BALLING: 1. vaginally implanted

12

cocaine. 2. having sexual intercourse.

BALL OF STRING, TO FEEL LIKE A: (Aus) tired out.

BALLOON: (US) 1. a small quantity of drugs wrapped in paper. 2. a heroin supplier. 3. a bar or saloon. A New York ordinance prohibited the word saloon on the fascia of a bar. In turn owners called them balloons.

BALLS: 1. testicles. 2. nerve, 'He's got the balls to do it.' 3. nonsense, 'You're talking balls.'

BAMBER, TO DO A: to make a mistake. UK police expression following an Essex murder investigation where some 20 mistakes resulted in a multiple homicide initially being thought to be murder and suicide. The name derives from Jeremy Bamber who in 1986 was sentenced to five terms of life imprisonment for the murder of five members of the family so, it was alleged, he could inherit his adoptive parents' fortune. The prosecution claimed he had misled the police into believing that his sister Sheila had killed her family and then committed suicide. His appeal was dismissed in March 1988 but he still maintains his innocence and is seeking to have his case referred back to the Court of Appeal.

BANANA RACE: (US) a fixed horse race.

BANANAS: 1. Special Patrol Group, 'They hang around in bunches and are yellow and bent.' 2. mad.

BANDIT: derisory UK police term for the small-time or unsuccessful thief, 'He's the world's premier gas-meter bandit.'

BANG: 1. to have sex. 2. to inject a drug. 3. inhalants. 4. (obs) to steal from a chain by breaking the holding ring with the thumb and forefinger. 5. to steal a purse. 6. an injection of narcotic taken intravenously and now subcutaneously to increase excitement. 7. excitement. 8. sexual intercourse. 9. a watch.

BANGED UP: 1. locked in a prison or police cell particularly on remand or awaiting sentence. 2. pregnant. 3. suffering from venereal disease.

13

BANGKOK CONNECTION: the drug route from Southeast Asia to Canada and the United States via Bangkok.

BANG TO RIGHTS: (UK) with no defence, *in flagrante delicto*, as in 'I've got to plead (guilty), I'm bang to rights.' Originally used in relation to theft, the phrase became a traditional one when, until the passing of the Police and Criminal Evidence Act 1985, verbals (qv) formed a major part of the case of the prosecution. Following the Act the phrase has become rarely heard in the courtroom itself.

BANG UP: excellent.

BANG, TO B. A HANGER: to steal a purse.

BANJO: 1. a prison loaf or cob used to make a sandwich in prisons before and shortly after World War Two. 2. any food stolen from the prison kitchen.

BAR: £1.

BARBARY COAST: (Aus) Elizabeth Street, Sydney, specifically from Campbell Street to Devonshire Street, known because of the number of neckings (qv) or robberies which took place in World War Two.

BARBECUE STOOL: (US) the electric chair.

BARBER: (Aus) to steal by stealth.

BARBERED BROADS: (Aus) playing cards with trimmed edges.

BARBS: barbiturates.

BARBUIT: a gambling game similar to craps.

BAREBACK RIDING: unprotected sex.

BAR L: Barlinnie Prison, Glasgow.

BARMY LANDING: the prison landing used for mentally disturbed prisoners, ex Barmy Park, an East End mental hospital.

BARNES MAN: a major drug dealer, ex the Harlem dealer Leroy 'Nicky' Barnes.

BARNYARD PIMP; (US) fried chicken, a staple part of the American prison diet.

BARON; 1. (US) a police officer assigned to a hotel beat. 2. (UK) a dealer in tobacco and now drugs in prison. A particularly powerful one can effectively control the inmates. At the time of the disturbances in Parkhurst Prison in 1969 the then baron had such control over the other prisoners that a film show could not start until he arrived. The role played by Noël Coward in *The Italian Job* may be an exaggeration but it is by no means a caricature.

BARONING; trafficking in prison.

BARREL MURDER; an early Mafia murder method in which the victim is nailed in a barrel and left to die. An example is the 1903 so-called Stable Murder at 323 E 10th, New York.

BASH; a smash and grab raid.

BASH, THE; prostitution.

BASKET; 1. an illegitimate child. 2. male genitalia.

BASKET LUNCH; fellatio.

BAT; (Aus) the penis.

BAT, TO GO OFF TO; (Aus) to masturbate.

BAT, TO GO ON A; to go on a spree drinking or whoring.

BATH, TO TAKE A; see take a bath.

BATO; (Sp. pris) a dude, friend, 'Hey, bato.'

BATPHONE; a policeman's mobile telephone, ex the strip cartoon character.

BATTER, ON THE; 1. to be engaged in prostitution ex 16c bat = prostitution. Now mainly North Country usage. A joke of the 1950s was Q. There are two flies on the roast beef and Yorkshire pudding. Which is the prostitute? A. The one on the batter. Green suggests it now applies to male prostitution. 2. (Scots) a drinking binge.

BATTY; 1. (Bl) the anus. 2. slightly mad.

BATTYMAN; (Bl) homosexual.

BAY STATE: (US) a hypodermic needle, ex the trade name.

BEACH, THE LATEST THING ON THE: (US) a new arrival in prison viewed from a sexual aspect.

BEAK: a judge or magistrate, ex the German Beck.

BEARD: a man possibly, but not necessarily, homosexual used to take out to dinner the wife of a man in prison. His function is that of a human chastity belt to prevent her becoming involved with other men.

BEARD, TO DON THE: (Aus) cunnilingus.

BEAST: 1. (WI) a police officer. 2. a sexual offender. Common in the North of England where the term nonce (qv) is not used.

BEASTMAN: (WI) police officer.

BEAT: (US) 1. to rob or mug. 2. to escape from prison.

BEAT DOWN: (US BI) a fight amongst prison inmates.

BEAUTY DOCTOR: (US) a steel-tipped club used to disfigure a victim.

BED AND BREAKFAST: half a crown. Pre-World War Two this was the price of a lodging.

BEEF: 1. (US) a charge. 2. to complain.

BEES: Beeswax = tax.

BEESMAN: (WI) police.

BEGGAR'S LAGGING: a three-month prison sentence being the standard penalty for begging. With the abolition in the 1980s of imprisonment for the offence the phrase is now obsolete.

BEGGING PONCE: a man who organises teams of beggars and takes a percentage of their earnings but who does not beg himself.

BELL: 1. to telephone. 2. a telephone call, ex the inventor Alexander Graham Bell.

BELLMAN: a specialist in cutting alarm systems.

BEND: 1. (US) to kill. (UK) 2. to

steal. 3. to distort, as in evidence.

BEND BACKWARDS, TO; to persuade a witness or defendant to change his mind yet again. This may occur when a witness displays an intention to give a statement contrary to the one first made by the police. He is then shown the error of his ways by the police who will point out the undesirability from everyone's point of view if this should happen and the unpleasantness this will cause him. It may also happen when a defendant decides to change his solicitor for another said to be able to obtain him bail or a certain acquittal. Rather than lose the client the first solicitor will endeavour to bend him backwards.

BENDER; 1. suspended sentence, ex suspender = bender. 2. a sustained drinking bout.

BENNIES; Benzedrine tablets.

BENT; 1. dishonest, as in lawyer or police officer. 2. stolen property, as in bent gear.

BENT, TO GO; to inform or to turn Queen's Evidence.

BERK; a foolish person, ex Berkley Hunt = cunt.

BERNIE; (US) a victim who might be armed and prepared to use the weapon, ex Bernard Goetz who killed a robber on the subway.

BERTIE, TO DO A; to inform on one's colleagues, ex the first modern London supergrass Bertie Smalls.

BEWER; a woman, no longer common but Irish tramp usage, poss. ex the Welsh bodyer = to feel.

B.F.; 1. (US) a pimp. 2. (UK) a bloody fool (euph).

B-GIRL; (US) a girl who works in a brothel where drinks are sold.

BICE; 1. a two-year sentence. £2, ex the French *bis* = twice.

BIDET; a rear wash wipe on a motorcar.

BIG C.; 1. a caution by the

police indicating that on an admission of guilt no further action will be taken. 2. cancer.

BIG GATES; (US) prison.

BIG GIRL; (Aus) an ounce of any prohibited but especially a hard drug.

BIG HOUSE; (US) State or Federal prison.

BIG JOHN; a police officer, no doubt from the name of some long-forgotten but then feared officer.

BIG ONE; 1. (US) $1,000. 2. (UK) £1,000. 3. death.

BIG ONE, TO GIVE IT THE; 1. to boast. 2. to intimidate.

BIG PAPA; the Thompson Machine Gun used in the Chicago gang wars.

BIG SLEEP; death.

BILL; the police. The origin of the word is open to many explanations, none of which is wholly satisfactory. One comes from the name of a policeman in the East End. When his dinner was ready his wife would send the daughter to enquire in local public houses if Old Bill was in. Another is that it comes from the character drawn by the First World War cartoonist Bruce Bairnsfather. A third that it refers to William IV, the reigning monarch when Sir Robert Peel's Metropolitan Police was formed in 1829.

BIN; 1. mental hospital. 2. prison cell. 3. (UK) a waistcoat pocket. 4. (US) a safe. 5. to lock up.

BING; (US) solitary confinement.

BINGLE; (Aus) a road traffic accident, usually a minor one.

BINO; (US) a prison riot.

BINS; 1. eyes. 2. binoculars.

BIRD; 1. a girl. 2. a prison sentence, ex birdlime = time. 3. (Aus) a horse running at long odds, abb. of dead bird. 4. (US gang) wine, ex Thunderbird, a cheap brand.

BIRD GAME, THE; theft of parrots and other expensive birds from pet shops or park aviaries by spraying them with Quick-Start. The spray knocked the birds out and they were then stuffed in the arms of puffa-jackets to be sold on South London estates. The Bird Game was regarded as an easy way for drug addicts to obtain quick money.

BIT; 1. a prison sentence, 'I did a six bit.' 2. an extra-marital girlfriend, 'I've got a bit on the side.'

BITCH; a woman to be avoided in a confidence trick as she may take the advice of her husband, 'Don't pitch to the bitch.'

BITCH, THE; (Can) an indefinite prison sentence.

BIT OF WORK; armed robbery.

BIZZY; see Busys.

BLACK BOOK; a book, often in code, kept by prostitutes containing names, addresses and predilections of clients. The book, which eliminates the need for street walking and other risky forms of contact, can be sold at a considerable price. In the wrong hands it becomes a weapon of blackmail.

BLACK MARIA; the van which took prisoners to jail. Another of the words with a variety of possible origins. Originally the van was black and had VR for Victoria Regina painted on it. The Ria comes from Victoria and the Ma may have been mother. An American version is that it derives from a black New York or Boston boarding house keeper who was called on by the police if they could not cope with a particularly difficult drunk. The third is that it was named after a Black prostitute who was a regular user of the van.

BLACK STUFF; opium.

BLACK, TO PUT THE B. ON; to blackmail.

BLADDER; (US) an unattractive prostitute.

BLADE; a knife.

BLAG; 1. to rob. 2. to borrow.

BLAG(GING); a robbery with violence.

BLAGGER; an armed robber, poss. ex blackguard.

BLAGUE, THE; specifically a smash and grab raid. Poss. ex the Fr *blague* = a confidence trick or abb. Eng. blackguard.

BLANK; to refuse, 'He wanted to borrow a grand but I blanked him out.'

BLANKET PARTY; (US) the practice by inmates of throwing a blanket over another, both to confuse and to avoid identification, prior to a beating or gang rape.

BLANKET TREATMENT, TO BE GIVEN THE; to receive a beating from prison officers.

BLAP UP; (UK Bl) to deceive with fast talk.

BLAT; 1. a newspaper, ex the German. 2. (Rus) a contact in the right place.

BLEAT; 1. a petition or appeal by a serving prisoner. 2. to inform or confess.

BLEED; to extort.

BLINDING; extremely good, a superlative, 'If I'd nicked the diamonds it would have been a blinding Christmas.'

BLIND PIG; an illegal drinking house, particularly during Prohibition.

BLISTER; 1. a summons to appear in court. 2. an endorsement on a driving licence.

BLITZ; to burgle or obtain entry to steal.

BLOCK; 1. (Can) solitary confine-ment in prison. 2. the head or brain, 'Use your block.' 3. to thwart or refuse as in an application for parole.

BLOOD; (US) name used amongst Black prisoners implying unity. The word can only be used by people of the same race.

BLOODCLAT; (Jam) untrustworthy, worthless, ex a santitary towel.

BLOOD IN, BLOOD OUT; only those who have taken a life may join a particular gang; only death will release them from membership.

BLOODS; a Californian street gang opposed to the Crips which now has nationwide ramifications.

BLOT; (Aus) the anus.

BLOW; 1. cannabis. 2. to leave a scene of crime before the arrival of the police. 3. to waste as in spending money recklessly. 4. to fail to take an opportunity, 'He blew a three-stroke lead going to the last.' 5. to fellate.

BLOW A PETER; to open a safe with explosives.

BLOW AWAY; to kill by shooting.

BLOWER; the telephone. Formerly the wire from a betting officer to a racecourse which enabled bookmakers to lay off bets which would result in too heavy a pay out and would help determine the starting price. In one of the great post-war racing coups a ringer (qv) was put in a race at Bath and the blower was cut to prevent the shortening of the starting price.

BLOWN; 1. to receive fellatio.

2. to have one's identity discovered.

BLOWN AWAY; killed.

BLOW-OFF; a tent at a carnival which will exhibit special acts such as the Fat Lady, the Woman with the Body of a Snake etc. Extra money will need to be paid to enter.

BLOW ONE DOWN; to kill.

BLOW ONE'S STACK; to lose one's temper.

BLOW THE GAFF; to inform.

BLOW THE WHISTLE; to inform.

BLUDGE; (Aus) to live off immoral earnings.

BLUDGER; (Aus) 1. a pimp. 2. a loafer. 3. a police officer. 4. a general term of opprobrium.

BLUE; (Aus) a fight.

BLUE BIRDS; thought to be the original name for the Aryan brotherhood prison gang.

BLUE COAT; a prisoner who had reached the second stage

after serving two and a half years of his sentence. He literally exchanged his grey coat for a blue one.

BLUE FOOT; (WI) a prostitute.

BLUEFLYER; a thief of lead, particularly from church roofs.

BLUE HEAVEN; the date-rape drug G.H.B.

BLUE PAPERS; the papers once sent to the prison authorities when a lifer was due for discharge or release in the next six months.

BLUE SKY; heroin.

BLUE TAB; (Can) a trusty prisoner, ex the band on his sleeve.

BLUEY; 1. lead, particularly from church roofs. 2. (Aus) a mate or friend, particularly red-haired. 3. a summons.

BOARDS; playing cards.

BOARDSMAN; a cardsharper, particularly a three-card trickster.

BOAT; 1. an elderly person in a

house to be burgled. 2. the face, boat race = face.

BOAT RACE; 1. a fixed sporting event. 2. the face.

BOBBING AND WEAVING; making a scratchy but not necessarily honest living, ex the action of a skilful boxer avoiding blows.

BOBBY; a police officer, ex Sir Robert Peel, the founder of the Metropolitan Police. An article in *Police Review* in 1960 suggested the word was then only used by tourists, e.g. Miller 'Bobbies on bicycles' in the song 'England Swings Like a Pendulum Do'. The usage seems to have made something of a comeback.

BOG-IE (-Y); 1. a police officer. 2. a police informer. 3. nasal mucus.

BOILED; drunk.

BOILER; a woman of mature years who dresses in a young style. Probably because an elderly hen has to be boiled rather than roasted to make it edible.

BOILERMAKER; (US) 1. a confidence trickster who has a way, particularly with middle-aged women. 2. beer with a whiskey chaser.

BOILER ROOM; a telephone call centre from which operators call potential clients inviting them to invest in fraudulent stocks and shares. Boiler rooms are often located in Southern California and Florida because of the accessibility of drugs. 'It's also a lot more fun to have $500,000 in Beverly Hills than it is in Bismark.'

BOLIVIAN MARCHING POWDER; cocaine.

BOLLOCKS; 1. testicles. 2. rubbish, 'What a load of bollocks.'

BOMB; 1. a large amount of money. 2. to fail. 3. (Aus) dope for a horse or greyhound.

BONE BOX; (US) a hearse, usually one taking away an inmate.

BONES; (US) an Afro-American.

BOOB; 1. a fool. 2. a police station or prison, abb. of booby hatch. By implication only fools would find themselves in one. 3. the female breast.

BOOBHEAD; (Aus) a prisoner shown respect by inmates and staff alike.

BOOBIES; 1. lice. 2. breasts.

BOOB TATTOO; (Aus) a tattoo between the shoulderblades, ex boobies, lice and therefore booby hatch.

BOOBY HATCH; 1. a police station. 2. a mental hospital. Cells were often infected with lice.

BOODLE; originally bad or counterfeit money now more usually stolen goods, ex the Dutch *boedel*.

BOOK; to charge a suspect with an offence.

BOOK, ON THE; to be on the Category A list of prisoners who would be a danger and embarrassment in the event of an escape.

BOOK, THE: the oral tradition of the rules of pimping.

BOOK, TO DO THE: to serve a life sentence.

BOOKS, THE: in Mafia circles when there is a vacancy the books are said to be open and when there is no recruiting the books are closed. Breach of this practice has led to innumerable quarrels and deaths.

BOOST: 1. to lift. 2. to steal, specifically to shoplift. 3. to induce a crowd to gamble or participate in, say, the purchase of counterfeit perfume and originally the work of a shill (qv).

BOOSTERS' DRAWERS: specially made underwear in which shoplifters put stolen goods.

BOOT: to smoke heroin through a foil tube, bootlace = chase (the dragon).

BOOT BURGLAR: a petty criminal who specialises in theft from car boots.

BOOT, TO PUT THE B. IN: to inflict severe and unnecessary punishment. This may be physical or verbal in e.g. the summing-up in a criminal trial adverse to the defence where the judge denigrates the defendant and his witnesses, 'He didn't half put the boot in.'

BOOTH: a member of the Salvation Army, ex the founder.

BOOTS: car tyres.

BOOTY: (Bl) the buttocks.

BOOTY BANDIT: (Bl) an active homosexual.

BORACIC: 1. impecunious, boracic lint = skint. 2. a tall story.

BORGATA: a crime family.

BOSS: (Aus) honorific term given to a warder below the rank of Assistant Superintendent.

BOSS OF BOSSES: a title reserved for the head of the most powerful (for the time being) of one of the five New York crime families.

BOT: (Aus) 1. tuberculosis. 2. a beggar.

BOTTLE; nerve, courage.

BOTTLE AND STOPPER; (US) police officer, bottle and stopper = copper.

BOTTLE GREEN AND LOUSY, TO BE; (Aus) to be in despair.

BOTTLE OF MILK; white with fear, 'He was so frightened he looked like a bottle of milk.'

BOTTLE OF SKINS; two elderly ladies, often sisters and spinsters, who have lived together throughout their lives. The word was specifically coined by a team of housebreakers in Darlington in the 1970s and has since passed into more general use in the North of England.

BOTTLE, ON THE; 1. an alcoholic. 2. a pickpocket. The word has been in use for over sixty years and is now most common amongst Black pickpockets on the underground.

BOTTLE, TO LOSE ONE'S B.; to lose one's nerve, bottle and glass = arse. Literally the person has fouled himself through fear.

BOTTLER; 1. a person who collects money for a busker. A bottle was used in preference to a hat or bag to prevent the spectators removing the takings. 2. (US) a girl who works in a brothel where drinks are sold.

BOUNTY BAR; see Coconut.

BOW; scrounging, abb. on the elbow.

BOW AND ARROW; (Can) position in which a prisoner is handcuffed with his hands behind his back and his ankles and hands joined.

BOWER BIRD; (Aus) a petty thief.

BOX; 1. a safe. 2. the vagina. 3. prison or police cell. 4. a coffin.

BOXCAR; a prison cell.

BOY BUSTER; (Aus) 1. a pederast 2. the seducer of young inmates.

BRACE; to grab, to confront.

BRACELETS; handcuffs.

BRAINS, THE: Criminal Investigation Department of Scotland Yard (derisory).

BRASCO: (Aus) a fairground lavatory.

BRASS: a prostitute, ex brass nail = tail.

BRASS CUPCAKE: something worthless.

BRASS EYE: (US) a prison cell which can only be unlocked electronically.

BRASSED-OFF, TO BE: to be annoyed. More common in the passive than in the active tense.

BRAT: (Aus) a young prisoner, specifically under 26.

BREAD: money. Not American as might be supposed but ex bread and honey = money.

BREAD AND BUTTER: a mental case, bread and butter = nutter.

BREAK A LEG: to lose one's virginity, now a theatrical wish of good luck.

BREAK WIDE: (US BI) to lose interest.

BREAST: (Aus) to accost.

BREEDER: (US) a heterosexual.

BREK: the last meal before the release of a prisoner. A few days before his release a con was able to say only 'four, three, two and a brek to go.' On the evening before his release both the prison officer and the prisoner would speak of having only time for a 'shit, shave and shampoo', cf. the naval 'Short sharp shit shave and shampoo ready for shore leave'. Like many older prison terms, brek has fallen into disuse.

BREW: illicit alcohol distilled in prison.

BRICK: (Aus) 1. ten years. 2. $10.

BRICKS, TO BE ON THE B.: (US) to be out of prison and on the streets again.

BRIDE: the feminine part of a lesbian relationship.

BRIDEWELL: 1. police cells. 2. (Liverpool) the charging officer.

BRIDGE: (Aus) a potential excuse.

BRIEF: 1. a lawyer, particularly a barrister, from the instructions given to him. 2. a driving licence. 3. a letter. 4. a cheque. 5. a search warrant.

BRIG: (US) prison ex Brit naval.

BROAD: (US) 1. woman. 2. a playing card. (UK) 3. identity or ration cards. 4. a credit card.

BROADSMAN: a cardsharper or three-card trickster.

BRONZE: faeces ex the colour.

BROWN BREAD: dead. One London criminal is known admiringly by his peers as Brown Bread Fred after the number of bodies, rightly or wrongly, attributed to him.

BROWN FOX: a sawn-off shotgun.

BROWN HATTER: a male, often rich, homosexual.

BROWN NOSE: to curry favour.

BROWN, TO GO IN THE: anal intercourse.

brush off

BROWN TROUT: (US) faeces.

BRUGAD: see Borgata.

BUBBLE: 1. to inform, ex bubble and squeak. 2. a Greek, ex the rhyming slang.

BUCK(ESS): (Liverpool) a young upwardly mobile criminal usually between the ages of 17 and 25, ex Irish, Bucko. Tony Barnes and ors, *Cocky,* 'It describes a young man, strong and lawless, who lives for the day and hangs the consequences. A buck trades on wild masculinity, gratuitous violence and contempt for social mores.'

BUCKET: 1. a motor car. 2. (Can) jail.

BUCKET SHOP: originally a shop dealing in stolen goods, the word has passed into common English as a place where discounted tickets can be purchased.

BUCKWHEAT: 1. to kill in a deliberately painful way. 2. abuse, overwork.

BUDGIE: a small-time police informer.

BUFF UP; (US) to put on muscle through excessive workouts in prison.

BUG; 1. to survey electronically. 2. (US) a criminal totally lacking in feeling.

BULGE, THE; an advantage, 'The boy has the bulge there.'

BULL; 1. a police officer, common amongst young West Indians. 2. (US) a prison guard.

BULLERMAN; (WI) a police officer.

BULLET; 1. (Aus) an Ace. 2. dismissal. 3. (US) 3. a one-year sentence. 4. a fast-rising record in the charts.

BULLPEN; (US) the reception area in a prison or police station.

BULLSEYE; 1. £50, ex the dartboard. 2. a policeman's lamp.

BUM; 1. (US) a tramp. 2. (UK) the buttocks. 3. to borrow with no intention of repaying the lender, 'Can I bum a fag off you?'

BUM BAY, TO DROP ANCHOR IN; anal intercourse.

BUM RAP; (US) a false allegation or charge which nevertheless is successfully proved.

BUMBLES; E. bumble bee = Ecstasy.

BUMMER; 1. a boring or unpleasant experience. 2. a homosexual.

BUMPER; (Aus) a cigarette end.

BUMP OFF; to kill.

BUNCO; (US) a confidence trick.

BUNG; a bribe.

BUNNY; 1. the victim of a confidence trick. 2. to talk indiscriminately and foolishly, to rabbit on. 3. foolish, 'Don't be a bunny.'

BURGLAR BRIGADE; prison officers who inspect the anal passage of a prisoner in search of contraband, particularly drugs.

BURIED, TO BE; 1. to receive a long prison sentence. 2. a bad fall in steeplechasing.

BURN; 1. roll-your-own prison

tobacco. 2. to die by electrocution. 3. to cheat. 4. to kill, specifically by shooting. 5. (UK) to open a safe with oxyacetylene.

BURNING COAL; (US pris) a sexual relationship between a black and a white man.

BURNT; 1. a window, burnt cinder = window. 2. to have contracted venereal disease.

BURTON, TO GO FOR A; to die, ex Burton on Trent = went.

BURY; 1. to sentence to imprisonment. 2. a bad fall in steeplechasing.

BUSH PAROLE; (US) to escape from prison.

BUSIES; the police, ex busybodies.

BUSINESS GIRL; prostitute.

BUSK; to improvise or pretend, 'How do we get in that house?' 'We'll busk it.'

BUSMAN; (Aus) one who breaks and enters a factory.

BUST; 1. to raid or arrest. 2. (Aus) to break and enter a factory.

BUSTER; (US gang) fake or imitation.

BUS THERAPY; (US pris) the practice of moving prisoners from one jail to another to keep them away from contacts, visits etc, cf. ghosting.

BUSTLE PINCHING (PUNCHING); frottage, the practice of rubbing against women in crowded places such as the underground.

BUST OUT; the forced bankruptcy of a person or organisation often caused through theft, fraud or extortion.

BUTTER AND EGG MAN; (US) a man, often elderly, from out of town with money to spend.

BUTTERED BUN, TO GO IN THE; to be the second man to have sexual intercourse.

BUTTERFLY; a young and pretty new arrival in prison.

BUTTON: (US) 1. a prison look-out. 2. the face, 'I gave him a poke in the button.'

BUTTONHOLE: (US) to recruit new members to a prison gang.

BUTTON MAN: (US) a foot soldier in the Mafia.

BUTTON UP: to stop betting or reduce stakes when winning.

BUY: to accept a story, particularly an untrue one.

BUYER: a receiver of stolen goods. Generally a thief can expect to receive one third of the value unless the goods have been specifically stolen to order.

BUZZ: 1. the pleasurable sensation from taking drugs. 2. to pick a pocket. Once a common word for thief, with moll buzzers = female pickpockets and kirk buzzers = those who stole from church congregations, the word has recently been more or less confined to the East End. 3. rumour, 'There's a buzz going round.'

C

C; 1. cocaine. 2. $100.

CABALLO; 1. heroin, ex Spanish *caballo* = horse. 2. someone who smuggles drugs into prison.

CABBAGE; money.

CABOOSE; buttocks.

CACHERO; (Sp pris) the dominant partner in a homosexual relationship.

CAD; 1. a rotter or low person. Said at one time to be a code for Constable in Disguise which would fit either of the foregoing. 2. (US) a ration of drugs, an abbreviation of Cadillac (qv).

CADILLAC; 1. (US pris) an ounce of heroin or, less usually, cocaine. 2. coffee with cream and sugar. 3. an officer's term for a vacant cell.

CAFONE; (US) a phoney, an embarrassment to himself and others.

CAGE; prison.

CAKE-HOLE; mouth, 'Shut your cake-hole.'

CAKE-O (BAKE-O); (pris) a person with plenty of something coveted by others.

CALABOOSE; (US) 1. prison, ex the Spanish *calabozo*. 2. a kitchen, ex ship's galley. Robert Hendrickson, *Word and Phrase Origins* suggests it is ex the Dutch *kombius* and travelled to America as the cook's wagon. 3. a motorcycle side car.

CALENDAR; one year's imprisonment.

CALLING CARD; (US) fingerprint, 'Mitt up (glove up) unless you want to leave your calling cards.'

CAN; 1. prison, from c.1930. 2. a lavatory, probably from mid 1940s. 3. a safe, c.1910, all need to be opened. 4. the buttocks c. mid 1930s presumably from 2. 5. an ounce of morphine. 6. the human head, c.1915, possibly a corruption of calabash, c.1850, meaning empty-headed. 7. to cease, to put an end to.

CANARY; a police informer. One of the foremost of informers against the Mafia was Abe 'Kid' Reles who was persuaded to turn against Albert Anastasia, Leo Lepke and a host of others from the notorious Murder Inc. of the 1930s. He was kept under police guard in an hotel in Brooklyn from which he apparently contrived to leap. There is little doubt he was thrown but, in Underworld circles, he became known as the 'canary who could not fly'. In early 19c slang a canary bird was a jail bird, a person kept in a cage.

CANARY, SING LIKE A; to confess to a crime or inform on one's colleagues.

CANDLE; a ponce, candle and sconce = ponce.

CANDY; 1. heroin. 2. anything very desirable, eg young men attractive to homosexuals.

CANDYLAND; Green Haven prison, New York.

CANDYMAN; originally specifically a heroin dealer but now more generally any drug dealer.

CANE; to smash or beat up. The word was often used in relation to stealing cars by smashing the quarterlight as in 'I caned it with a stone.' It was also applied to stealing car radios.

CAN-HOUSE; brothel.

CANNED; drunk.

CANNED GOODS; a virgin.

CANNISTER; 1. a revolver. 2. a jail. 3. a safe. 4. the buttocks.

CANNON; a pickpocket.

CANNON, THE; the pickpocket trade. Criminal offences were often given titles as in The Life (qv).

CAP; 1. narcotics in capsule form. 2. to have oral sex. 3. to kill.

CAPER; a theft or robbery.

CAPPING; (US pris) talking about one's family or friends in a disrespectful way.

CAPO(REGIME): ranking member of a crime family who has a crew.

CAPODECINA: ranking member of a crime family who heads a crew of ten.

CARD, GO THROUGH THE: to cover comprehensively, ex backing every winner on a race card.

CARD, HAVE ONE'S C. MARKED: to be given inside information, possibly by a corrupt policeman, of an impending raid or possibly of the availability of stolen goods. The phrase originates from the marking of a race card by a tout, pretending to have inside information from a stable of the certain prospects of a horse. In addition to the money paid to the tout there would be a request for a smaller sum 'for the stable lad', the non-existent person who had allegedly supplied the information. The exercise was a classic example of the working of the short con (qv).

CARE BEAR: a social worker, ex the film *The Care Bears*.

CARGA: (Sp pris) heroin.

CARJACK: the theft of cars from their owners at gun or knife point, very common in South Africa and the US and increasing in Britain.

CARLA ROSA: fraud, deceit, someone who is not what he or she seems, ex the opera company Carla Rosa = poser.

CARNAL: (Sp pris) a trusted friend.

CAR PARK: a police informer, car park = nark.

CARPET: 1. three months' imprisonment. It was said to take ninety days to weave a carpet on the prison loom. Also poss. ex carpet bag = drag. Dragging (qv) often attracted a sentence of three months. 2. £3. 3. a pull on a cigarette. 4. a nuisance. 5. (US) a meeting of at least two Mafia families with the intention of resolving interfamily disputes.

CARPEY: to be locked in a prison cell for the night, ex the Latin *carpe diem*.

CARVE UP: to share the proceeds of a robbery or other ill-gotten gains.

CASE: 1. to watch. 2. to reconnoitre a location prior to a robbery or burglary. 3. a brothel.

CASE, TO GO: to sleep with a usually unspecified woman, 'Were you working last night?' 'No, I was going case.'

CASE DOUGH: (US) a nest egg, in theory an untouchable money reserve.

CASEKEEPER: a brothel keeper.

CASER: five shillings.

CASH IN ONE'S CHIPS: to die, ex returning gaming chips in a casino.

CAT: 1. a thief with an iron nerve as in cat burglar. The implication is that he is as agile and cold blooded as a cat. 2. the cat-o'-nine-tails, the whip used in a prison flogging, see also pussy. 3. a young homosexual, abb. catamite. 4. a prostitute. 5. (US Bl) c.1900, a man dressed in the latest fashion who pursues women. 6. a jazz musician.

CATCH: to receive anal intercourse.

CATCH A COLD: to lose a considerable sum of money gambling.

CATCH A SQUARE: to get ready to fight, ex boxing.

CATCH A STACK: (US) to rob someone of a substantial sum of money.

CATCH COLD: (US) to be killed.

CATCHER: a passive homosexual.

CATCH OUT: (US) to request protective custody in prison cf. Rule 43.

CAT-CROOK: (US) a poor quality crook cf. International gas-meter bandit.

CATFISH DEATH: (US) suicide by drowning.

CATHAUL: (US) prolonged

questioning of a suspect, ex the 19c practice of dragging a clawing cat up the suspect's bare back.

CATHOUSE: (US) a brothel, ex the enthusiasm of tomcats for sexual intercourse.

CATTED, TO BE: to be allocated a category in prison. A Category A prisoner is regarded as a potential danger to the public and an escape liability. They are placed in patches (qv). In theory as the prisoner serves his sentence he goes through the categories, reaching D which will mean transfer to an open prison and outside work prior to his release.

CATTLE, TO: 1. to have sexual intercourse, ex cattle truck = fuck. 2. to defeat or swindle, 'That cattled him.'

CAT-UP: (US) a robbery with a gun.

CAT WAGON: a mobile brothel which catered for itinerant workers in rural America. The less well off would have to make do with an inflatable dummy.

CATWEED: marijuana.

CEMENT COFFIN: the method of killing a victim by placing his body, or his feet, in cement until it hardens. He is then drowned. Also known as a cement overcoat or cement shoes.

CHAIR, THE: the electric chair. Invented in the 1880s in America as a humane way of carrying out the death penalty.

CHAIRMAN: an adviser to La Cosa Nostra.

CHAIRMAN OF THE BOARD: the highest-ranking member of a crime family; in recent years specifically Jack Tocco in Detroit.

CHALK: (US) to distract a prison officer so another prisoner may escape or break rules.

CHANT: to blackmail, ex Fr. *chantage*.

CHANTA: (Sp) a prison cell, literally house.

CHAP: in-house term for a professional criminal. Marilyn Wisbey,

Gangsters Moll, 'Top of the league would be security van robbers, train robbers, bank robbers, city financial scams and jewellery robbers. ... Second would be top-class shoplifters, hi-jackers and credit card frauds. Lastly, you'd have fences, spivs and unlicensed street traders.'

CHAPPER: a police officer, ex Yiddish.

CHARGE: cannabis.

CHARLIE: 1. cocaine 2. (Aus) a prostitute. 3. the female breast. 4. a policeman, ex the night watchman in the reign of Charles II.

CHARLIE BIG SPUDS: a braggart or someone who thinks they are something above their actual station.

CHARLIE WOOD: see Wood, Charlie.

CHASED, TO BE: to be exiled from, rather than killed by, a Mafia family. The person may no longer undertake business with a made man (qv).

CHASE THE DRAGON: to sniff heroin by burning the drug on foil and inhaling through a tube. Thought to be safer than injecting.

CHATS: (Aus) lice.

CHAVA: (Sp pris) a wimp.

CHAW: to arrest, particularly pickpockets on the underground.

CHAWRY GOODS: stolen property, poss. ex the Hindi via the Romany.

CHEATERS: loaded dice or marked cards.

CHECK COP: adhesive paste on the palm so when a cheat puts his hand on a stack of chips the top one will stick.

CHEDAR: a prison cell, ex Jewish, a small room or study.

CHEESE: a girlfriend, ex cheese and kisses = missus.

CHEESEBOX: the State Correctional Facility at Joliet, Ill.

CHERRIES: greyhounds, cherry hogs = dogs.

CHERRY; 1. the vagina or anus. 2. an apprentice jockey.

CHERRY, TO BE; virgin, unsoiled.

CHICAGO LEPROSY; (US) sores resulting from the use of hypodermic needles.

CHICAGO OVERCOAT; a coffin.

CHICAGO PIANO; the Thompson Machine Gun used in the Chicago gang wars during Prohibition. The weapon, which fired up to a thousand .45 bullets a minute, originally cost less than $200.

CHICKEN HAWK; a homosexual who seeks out under-age boys. The celebrated lawyer and Master of University College, Oxford, Lord Goodman, obtained substantial damages from a magazine over allegations that he was a chicken hawk.

CHICKEN RANCH; generically a brothel. It specifically referred to a brothel in La Grange, Texas, which was in existence in one form or another until its closure in 1973.

CHICKEN SCRATCH; the prac-

tice of a drug addict crawling on the floor in the hope of finding specks of drugs, particularly crack.

CHIEF CORRUPTER; the member of a crime family whose specific task is to attempt the bribery of politicians.

CHILDREN; housebreaking equipment; Boys and girls = twirls (qv).

CHILL; to kill, ex the cold of a dead body.

CHILL TOWN; Long Island or Coney Island, New York.

CHINAMAN'S CHOICE; no choice at all.

CHIP; to carry out petty crimes.

CHIP DOG; a gang member who skims money or drugs.

CHIPPING; a version of the corner game. A girl pretends to be a prostitute and disappears with the cash before sex can take place.

CHIPPY; 1. to have sexual

chicken feed

intercourse. 2. a young girl, sometimes but not necessarily a prostitute. 3. a victim of a confidence trick. 4. aggressive behaviour.

CHIRULIN: (Hisp pris) a police informer. [pron. Cheer-u-lean]

CHIV: a cut-throat razor, knife or other sharp weapon, including a home-made one, for cutting or stabbing, ex the 18c English to chive, meaning to cut, ex Romany. Chiv, however, seems to have been an American import at the end of the 19c.

CHIVING: 1. to slash with, or a slash with, a razor or knife. In the 1920s this was specifically to cut with broken glass and was used at race tracks in the quarrels between the Sabini brothers and the Brummagem boys for control of bookmakers' pitches all over England. See also Glassing. 2. to saw, 'I chived the darbies' = 'I cut off the handcuffs.'

CHOCOLATE FREEWAY: the anus.

CHOIRBOYS: (US) rookie i.e. newly recruited police officer.

Joseph Wambaugh, *The Choirboys*.

CHOIR PRACTICE: an informal meeting of police officers after duty for drink and sex.

CHOKE (STRANGLE) A DARKIE, TO: (Aus) to defecate, ex the Barry McKenzie 1960s strip cartoon.

CHOKE, TO: 1. to bribe fr. c.1925. 2. to stop a racehorse from winning and therefore 3. to seize up when in a winning position. 4. (US) to extinguish, 'Choke that glim (flashlight).'

CHOKED, TO BE: upset, annoyed, 'I wasn't half choked when I got that pull.'

CHOKER: 1. the gallows at Newgate prison (Fr. mid-19c). 2. a hangman. 3. a garotter. After the Crimean War when a number of soldiers were discharged garotting became very popular as a form of robbery, particularly in London. 4. a clergyman's collar. 5. a white scarf worn by costermongers. 6. (US) a pickpocket. 7. a sportsperson who seizes up when in a winning

chiselers

position, e.g. Jana Novotna when in a seemingly impregnable position at Wimbledon. 8. (tramp) cheese, because it can stop diarrhoea.

CHOK(E)Y: 1. (Aus) prison generally (Naval c.1850), prob ex 17c Hindi *chauki*, a four-sided place, subsequently a police station. 2. the punishment cell of a prison.

CHOLO: (US) a member of the same gang.

CHO MO: (US) a child molester.

CHOPPER: 1. a machine gun. 2. a helicopter. 3. the penis. *Chopper* by the Australian criminal Mark Read refers, however, to the self-mutilation of his ears. 4. a motorbicycle.

CHOPPERS: 1. the teeth. 2. the plural of the above.

CHORE: to steal, ex Romany.

CHOW: 1. food 2. tobacco, ex chewing or chawing a piece of tobacco.

CHRISTER: an evangelist, often born again, and often one in charge of food distribution at a mission where religion is an integral part of the diet.

CHRISTINE: crystal methamphetamine.

CHRISTMAS HOLD: (Aus) grabbing the testicles.

CHUBB: to lock, ex the locksmith.

CHUCK: (US) a White prisoner or officer.

CHUCKED, TO BE: 1. to be acquitted. 2. to be rejected by a lover.

CHUCKS: the martial arts weapon nunchucks. In prison nunchucks are generally made by joining cut sections of broom handles 6 to 12 inches long with leather laces or shoestring.

CHUMMY: anyone of whom a police officer is speaking but usually a suspect, 'Chummy did a runner.'

CIRCUS: a sexual exhibition performed in a brothel.

CIVILIAN: a person who is neither a policeman nor a working criminal.

CLARET: blood. Although often used as a euphemism in boxing writing, the word is particularly common in South London where it is not always used in connection with the sport. Dekker 1604, 'my head runs claret lustily'.

CLEAN: 1. free from drugs, a gun or stolen property when tested or searched. 2. a person with no criminal convictions.

CLEAN SKIN: (Aus) no criminal record.

CLEAN SNEAK: a successful job with no clues as to the perpetrator left behind. More difficult in these days of DNA.

CLEAN WHEELS: a motor car, which has not previously come to the notice of the police, used in a crime.

CLEARING HOUSE: (US) a system which ensures all bets taken by bookmakers. In England the system is called laying off.

CLICK ON: (US) an attack by two or more prisoners on a single inmate, 'They clicked on me.'

CLIMBER: a burglar who literally climbed up the outside of buildings, particularly hotels. The great climbers of the second half of the 20c included George 'Taters' Chatham, Ray 'The Cat' Jones and Peter Scott. All are dead or retired. A climber would normally be slightly built but Scott was a noted exception with enormous strength in his upper arms.

CLINK: prison, ex the debtors' prison in Clink Street, South London.

CLINKERS: (Aus) 1. pellets of faeces adhering to anal hair, orig. 19c English. 2. irons worn by prisoners 3. a crafty fellow.

CLIP: 1. to kill. 2. to cheat, usually of no great amount and specifically by a prostitute who cheats a client out of the sex act.

CLIP JOINT: a low drinking club, dance hall or bar where the victim will be clipped, i.e. led on to think he and the hostess are drinking champagne when the management is serving lemonade. It is not necessary that sexual services are offered but it is the intention that the visitor should think so.

CLOCK: 1. the face. 2. to recognise. 3. to watch. 4. to hit. 5. to count money. 6. (US) to time a racehorse in its work. 7. (Aus) twelve months' imprisonment.

CLOCK, TO CHOP THE: to turn back the miles on a car's odometer.

CLOTHESLINER: 1. derogatory term for any petty criminal, originally one who stole washing. 2. a blow across the throat delivered with a straight arm.

CLOUT: 1. influence. 2. the vagina, poss. ex the influence it may have. 3. to hit. 4. to steal.

CLOUT AND LAM: literally to steal and run, ex 18c clout, a handkerchief of which there was a ready market for stolen ones.

CLOUTING: 1. originally stealing handkerchiefs but later theft in general. 2. the delivery of hard blows.

CLUBHOUSE: (US) a police station.

CLUB NUMBER: the Criminal Record Office number of a person convicted of a previous offence. Usually only the last three are read out in court on conviction unless the same sort of offence appears earlier in the record.

CLUCK: 1. to crave drugs. 2. a cocaine customer.

CLUCKING: withdrawing from drugs.

CLUMPER: an enforcer in the Timeshare trade.

CLUMPING: the beating given to a late payer.

COAT: 1. (US) $100 given as a bribe to a police officer. 2. a suspect, 'Have you got a coat?' 3. to tell off or scold, 'I gave him a right coating.'

COB: a prison loaf which could be used to make a sandwich.

COBBLERS: 1. testicles, cobbler's awls = balls. 2. money. 3. rubbish, 'You're talking a load of cobblers.'

COBBLES, ON THE: streetfighting without weapons.

COCER: (Sp pris) an inmate on death row awaiting electrocution.

COCK: 1. a person, often a publican or scrap metal dealer, invited by a police officer to a function in the certain knowledge that the cock will pay for the evening's entertainment. The cock knows this and will oblige in return for future unspecified favours such as the warning of an impending search for stolen property. Poss. ex cock and hen = ten, the cost long ago of a night out. 2. the penis 3. the female genitals, used in Black pimp slang.

COCK AND HEN: 1. £10. 2. a sentence of ten years' imprisonment.

COCKATOO: (Aus) the look-out in a Two-up school (qv).

COCKY WATCHMAN: the best.

Mainly Liverpudlian use and abbreviated to Cocky. A term of approbation applied to the major Liverpool drug dealer, Curtis Warren.

COCOA, TO COME HIS: 1. to ejaculate. 2. to confess.

COCONUT: a term of racial abuse amongst West Indians suggesting pro-White feelings — brown outside, white inside.

CODIE: a child molester.

COLD BISCUIT: a prostitute's unattractive client or one difficult to arouse.

COLD DECK: a deck of cards previously stacked in a certain order to be switched during play for another pack.

COLD STORAGE: (US pris) solitary confinement.

COLD TURKEY: a hard way of coming off a drug addiction without supportive medicine such as methadone or tranquillisers. One of the side effects is that the skin becomes pimpled like that of a turkey or goose.

COLLAR: 1. a policeman. 2. an arrest. 3. to make an arrest. 4. non-criminal 9 to 5 work.

COLLAR, TO HAVE ONE'S C. FELT: to be arrested.

COLLEGE: prison, in UK specifically Borstal, a penal system devised for young offenders based on a college education; in US a state prison or penitentiary.

COLLEGE STREET SOLICITOR: (Aus) male prostitute, ex an area of Hyde Park, Sydney.

COLOURFUL RACING IDENTITY: (Aus) a criminal, abb. to colourful identity or identity, fr. c.1860 when identity meant a long standing resident.

COMARE: the girlfriend or mistress of a gangland figure.

COME CLEAN: to confess, Graham Greene, 'Baines coming clean', *The Fallen Idol*.

COME HEAVY: (US) to arrive carrying a loaded gun.

COMP: (US) a waitress or croupier required by the management to sleep with the high-rolling punter at a casino.

COMPARE: the associate or friend of a crime figure, ex Sp Compadre.

COMPUESTO: (Sp pris) shooting drugs, usually heroin.

CON: 1. a prisoner, ex convict. 2. a trick, ex confidence trick. 3. to swindle or cheat.

CONCAVES: (Aus) trimmed playing cards.

CONDY BOY: (Aus) a cleaner in a brothel. Condy's crystals dissolved in water were a popular vaginal douche.

CONFUSION: (WI) a street fight.

CONNECTED, TO BE: a person who does business with the Mafia without being a member is said to be connected.

CONNECTION: 1. an arrangement with a supplier of drugs. 2. the relationship of a minor criminal with a major one who, in return for services rendered, will protect him from the predations of other criminals and, to an extent, the police.

CONS; the previous convictions of a prisoner.

CONSIGLIERE; the adviser, possibly but not necessarily of a crime family.

CONTRACT; a purchased killing.

CONVICT; a prisoner who maintains his values, a term of admiration not given to an inmate.

COOKIES; 1. a prize in the form of money or sex 2. to vomit, 'He chucked his cookies.'

COOL; 1. a term of approbation. 2. to knock out.

COOLER; (US) 1. prison, particularly solitary confinement. 2. a woman.

COON; an Afro-American, ex their supposed taste for racoon meat.

COONEH; a fool or possible mark, ex Yiddish.

COOPING; the practice of a

uniformed police officer sleeping whilst on duty.

COP; 1. a police officer. 2. to obtain, take possession of. 3. to obtain a woman for a pimp's stable. 4. to arrest. 5. to receive something, generally unpleasant, 'I copped a blister (qv).' 'He copped a seven.' 6. to steal.

COPACETIC; (US BI) safe or clear, popularised by the dancer Bill 'Bojangles' Robinson, ex Yiddish, *kopasectic*.

COP A HEEL; (US) to escape from prison.

COP A JOINT; to practise oral sex.

COP A KNOCKER; (US) to be arrested, mainly vagrant usage.

COP A LIE (DOWN); to receive a sentence of imprisonment.

COP A MOKE; (US) to escape from prison.

COP AND BLOW; (US BI) obtaining money from a prostitute who is not regarded as a long-term member of a stable by working her hard in the short term.

COP A PLEA: to plead guilty in the hope and expectation of a lesser sentence. In England and Wales generally the earlier a plea of guilty is entered in the proceedings the bigger the discount on the sentence.

COP KILLER: (US) a bullet capable of penetrating a 'bullet-proof' vest.

COPPER'S NARK: a regular police informer.

COPPERTIME: (US) time off for good behaviour.

COPPING DEUCES: (US) to change one's mind, cf a touch of seconds.

COP SHOP: a police station.

COP SOME ZZZS: (Bl) to sleep.

COP SOP: false name given on arrest.

CORN: 1. a large sum of money. 2. Bourbon whiskey, ex corn liquor.

CORNER: 1. a share in the proceeds of crime. This is not necessarily an equal share but may depend on the part played. The driver in a wages snatch might not necessarily receive the same as one of the men across the pavement. The man who provided a stolen car for the operation certainly would not. 2. To sell shoddy goods pretending they are high class.

CORNER GAME: to sell genuinely stolen goods to a tradesman and then have him arrested by others pretending to be police officers. For a sum of money and the loss of goods the victim believes he has avoided prosecution.

COSH: 1. a weighted object. 2. to hit with a weighted object, ex Romany, *koshter* = a stick.

COSH, TO BE UNDER THE: to be in another's power; to do their bidding.

COTTAGE: a public lavatory, often a homosexual meeting place.

COTTAGING: the practice of

males frequenting public lavatories seeking casual sex.

COUGH: to confess, 'He wouldn't cough if he had bronchitis.'

COUNTRY, THE: Dartmoor prison.

COUP, THE: What is happening? 'What's the coup?'

COURTING IN: the initiation process for gang membership. The inductee must fight two or more members for a set number of seconds usually between 15 and 30.

COWBOY: 1. a fast and reckless losing gambler. 2. a reckless thief or one who unnecessarily hurts his victims. 3. (US) a new or inexperienced prison officer. As backslang Yobwoc it translates as 'Young, obnoxious bastard we often con.'

COW'S CALF: ten shillings, cow's calf = half.

COYOTE: 1. a transporter of illegal immigrants across the Mexican border. 2. an extremely ugly woman. A coyote will bite off his leg in a trap. If he finds her head on it, the man will bite off his arm rather than wake the woman in the morning.

COZZER: a police officer, ex copper and rozzer.

CRAB: (US) to solve.

CRACK: 1. cocaine baked into crystals. Smoked it produces a fast high and in turn is highly addictive. 2. the vagina. 3. (US) an insulting remark. 4. an enjoyable time, ex Irish *craic*. 5. to confess, particularly under pressure such as the threat to charge a wife or girlfriend.

CRACK A LAY: the art of the housebreaker.

CRACKERS: (Aus) a brothel.

CRACKSMAN: 1. a safebreaker. The art of the safebreaker, once the aristocrat of the prison hierarchy, has been rendered almost useless by the introduction of modern technology and the reluctance of the modern criminal to serve an apprenticeship. 2. a drug taker, esp. crack cocaine. Dave Courtney, 'The average cracksman has to find £500 a day to feed his habit. He has to go out and rob.'

CRACK THE WORKS; to inform to the police.

CRAP; 1. to defecate, ex Thomas Crapper the inventor of the modern flushing lavatory. It is said that a design of a rudimentary version of the water closet was shown to Queen Elizabeth I. The inventor had, however, decorated the design by having carp or goldfish in the water. The project came to nothing. 2. poor quality goods. 3. nonsense, 'That's a load of crap.'

CRASH; 1. to sleep, particularly a police officer on duty. 2. to write off an offence thought to be more trouble than it is worth, e.g. domestic violence. Crashing is one of the many problems of obtaining accurate statistics of crime.

CREAM; to steal from an employer.

CREEPER; a hotel or house burglar who will work with the victim in the room. In some instances a creeper will work with a prostitute who will occupy the client whilst he empties the man's pockets.

CREEPING AND TILLING; (US BI) stealing from shop tills.

CREW; a Mafia unit working under a street captain.

CRIB; 1. originally a prostitute's room but now more generally an apartment or flat. 2. a safe.

CRIMP; (US) to inform.

CRIPS; Southern Californian street gang opposed to the Bloods. Originally to be a member an initiate had to kill or maim another individual. The gang now has affiliations throughout the US.

CRO; Criminal Records Office but more usually referring to the Form 609 on which a criminal record is contained.

CROAK; to die.

CROAKER; 1. a professional killer. 2. a doctor, specifically a prison doctor. 3. a police informer. 4. someone who forecasts ill fortune, ex the croak of a raven, a supposed bird of ill omen.

CROMO: (Aus) a prostitute, ex Brett Harris' description of a prostitute who was painted to look like a chromolithograph rather than the original.

CROSS-BAR HOTEL: prison.

CROSS-COUNTRY CHASER: (US) the military equivalent of a bounty hunter assigned to bring back AWOL marines. See Joe Jackson and William Burke jnr., *Dead Run*.

CROSS-HAND BOOGIE: mutual masturbation.

CROW: (Aus) 1. a look-out man in a three-card trick. 2. strictly a prostitute but now in more general usage as girlfriend. There are a number of variations, e.g. society crow, bed and breakfast crow, charity crow.

CROWN AND ANCHOR: a gambling board game played outside greyhound tracks etc. The punter has no more chance of winning than he does at Find the Lady.

CRUDE: a tip off by a police informer rather than one by a member of the general public.

CRULLER: the head.

CRUMPET: a woman seen in sexual terms.

CRUSHER: a policeman, ex beetle crusher.

CRUSHING: the police practice of disregarding a complaint.

CRUST: the head, ex crusted bread = head.

CRUST, OUT OF HIS: out of his mind.

CRUTCHING: smuggling drugs into prison in the vagina. The drugs are often enclosed in a condom and are then concealed by a tampon.

CUFF: 1. to handcuff. 2. to write off an offence rather than charge a suspect. 3. (US) to swindle, especially on an instalment plan. 4. to defer payment, often with the intention of avoiding it completely.

CUFF, ON THE; obtaining goods on credit.

CUFFING; see crushing.

CUGINE; 1. a small-time thief. 2. a person to be inducted into the Mafia.

CULL; an honest man, a dupe.

CUM CHUM; (US pris) a passive homosexual.

CUPCAKES; (US pris) a passive homosexual.

CURBING; late 18c word for stealing with a pole from open windows.

CUSH; savings, something to fall back on, ex cushion.

CUT; 1. to slash with a razor. 2. (US) the area around a prison bed or bunk considered that person's territory.

CUT DOWN; to kill, particularly by shooting.

CUT OFF AT THE KNEES, TO BE; to be left without a remedy or option.

CUT OUT; (Aus) to serve a period of imprisonment rather than pay a fine.

CUTTING GEAR; oxyacetylene equipment used for safebreaking.

CUT UP TOUCHES; to reminisce.

C.W.; a co-operating witness.

D

DAB: fingerprint.

DABBLER: an occasional user of heroin or other drugs.

DAD: (US pris) a homosexual's lover who owns him and is expected to protect him.

DAG: (Aus) 1. an extrovert person. 2. the wool-encrusted faeces hanging from the backside of a sheep.

DAIRY: suspicion, 'I only did that to take the dairy off myself.' Poss. dairy cream = beam = spotlight.

DAISY CHAIN: homosexual group sex. With careful timing a mass mutual orgasm can be achieved.

DANCE: to steal from the upper floors of buildings, ex 17c dance = staircase.

DANCE FLOOR: the condemned cell, ex the continuing pacing of the prisoner.

DANCER: a cat burglar.

DANGLER: (Aus) an indecent exposer.

DA PROJECTS: Sing Sing prison.

DARBIES: 1. originally fetters now handcuffs. 2. the iron clad terms of a moneylender.

DARBY: 1. money. 2. the stomach, ex Darby Kelly = belly.

DASH: originally a gratuity now a bribe.

DATASTREAMING: a form of credit card fraud in which a hacker obtains credit card details from high street retailers and then creates counterfeit cards to be used abroad. *Sunday Times*, 26 August 2001, 'Datastreaming, a new and fast growing crime'.

DAUB: 1. fingerprint. 2. an identifying mark made on a playing card by a cheat.

DEADBEAT: (US) one who borrows with no intention of repaying a loan.

DEAD COPPER; (Aus) an informer.

DEAD CRIMINAL; a retired or, worse, a reformed one.

DEAD END STREET; (Can) the female pudenda.

DEAD HOUSE; a low dive.

DEAD LEVEL; honest.

DEAD MAN'S SHIRT; a shirt given to a prisoner on his release, traditionally believed to have come from another who died in prison.

DEAD PICKING; stealing from drunks.

DEAD PIGEON; one against whom the evidence is overwhelming.

DEAD PRESIDENTS; money.

DEAF AND DUMB; the anus, ex deaf and dumb = bum.

DEAL; 1. a plea bargain in which a shorter or non-custodial sentence will be imposed in return for a plea of guilty. The prosecution may also drop more serious charges. 2. to trade in narcotics 3. (SA) to cheat.

DEANER; one shilling.

DEAR JOHN; a letter sent to a prisoner indicating a relationship has ended, 'Dear John, I have met this other man and am having his baby ...'

DECK; 1. a pack of cards 2. to knock down.

DECKO (DEKKO); to look or spy, ex Urdu, 'Have a dekko at this.'

DEEP SEA DIVER OR FISHERMAN; a cardsharp on an oceangoing liner. The victim would be set up for one last big game shortly before the boat docked. All his prior winnings and a considerable sum in addition would go to the sharps. When the Assistant Chief Inspector John L. Sullivan commented to one of the gambler and con man Nicky Arnstein's potential victims that he should surely know he was about to be fleeced, he received the reply, 'Of course I know but he's better company than the honest men on board this ship.'

DEEP SIX: to kill, ex naval in which unwanted items were thrown overboard when they would drop to six fathoms.

DEPS: depositions taken in criminal cases in magistrates' courts to establish whether the prosecution has made a *prima facie* case on which to commit the prisoner to jury trial.

DESERT, THE: Queens, New York.

DEUCE: a two-year prison sentence.

DIAMOND: 1. term of approval, 'He's a real diamond.' 2. East End Jewish prostitute, ex play on words, Koh-I-Noor = Cohen whore.

DIBBLE: a police officer, ex the cartoon character in *Top Cat*.

DICK(S): 1. police officer(s), ex 16c a simpleton. 2. head or body lice. 3. the penis, dickory dock = cock.

DICKLESS TRACEY: (Aus) a

policewoman or traffic warden, ex the strip cartoon.

DIDDIKOI: a gypsy, strictly a half Romany.

DIDDLER: (US/Can) sex offender.

DIDO: an internal police complaint, i.e. not one made by a member of the public.

DIESEL: 1. a cup of prison tea. 2. a lesbian, abb. diesel dyke.

DIG: 1. a punch. 2. to understand or appreciate, 'Do you dig it?'

DIGGER: 1. (Can) punishment cell. 2. (Army) table knife. 3. an Australian.

DIG OUT: to victimise in prison.

DIHEDRAL: the degree of dishonesty in a prison officer, ex RAF, 'What's his dihedral?'

DIME: (US) 1. Ten years' imprisonment. 2. to inform, ex the practice of dropping coins near the body of a killed informer, e.g. Frank Bompensiero shot at a telephone kiosk in San Diego on 10 February 1977.

DIP: a pickpocket.

DIP, THE: the part of Piccadilly adjoining St James's Park where male prostitutes importuned wealthy homosexuals.

DIRTY: (US) carrying drugs or illegal weapons.

DIRTY DISHES: false evidence.

DIS(S): 1. (Bl) to show disrespect, 'He dissed me so I striped him.' 2. (Aus) discarding one from a pair of dice and substituting a crooked one.

DISH OUT THE PORRIDGE: to pass a heavy sentence.

DISNEYLAND: (US) an easy prison in which to serve a sentence.

DISTRESS: to carry out a mass robbery often on the underground or train where a group will take over a carriage and systematically rob the passengers.

DISTRICT MAN: (US) a crime family member who controls a small urban area.

DIV: 1. a stupid person. 2. a weak prisoner, poss. ex Romany *divio* = mad.

DIVE: a low drinking place.

DIVE, TO TAKE A: deliberately to lose a boxing contest. This can be done either for betting purposes or to enhance the reputation of a local hero.

DIVER: pickpocket, see Jenny Diver, *The Threepenny Opera*.

DIVOT: toupee.

DIXIE CUP: (US) a hired killer who will then be killed by his employer, ex the disposability of a Dixie cup, a cardboard container.

D. MECCA: (US gang) Detroit.

DO: 1. to kill. 2. to beat up badly. 3. to commit a theft. 4. to search (esp. police). 5. to swindle or cheat.

D.O.A.: dead on arrival at hospital.

DO A RUNNER: 1. to escape from the police following a crime. 2. to abscond bail.

DO A SLAMMER: to be cautioned by the police as a juvenile.

DOB IN: (Aus) to inform.

DODGY: slightly dishonest.

DOG: 1. an unpleasant or sadistic man, e.g. a judge who hands out a savage sentence and so is termed 'a right dog'. 2. an unattractive woman. 3. the telephone, ex dog and bone = phone. 4. a cigarette. 5. to follow. 6. (jam) a gun.

DOG, TO KEEP: to keep look out in three-card trick and so warn of the arrival of police.

DOG, TO TURN: (Aus) to inform.

DOG DRIVER: (WI) a police officer.

DOG-EYE: the look-out man in a three-card trick game.

DOG FOOD: (US) heroin.

DOGGY FASHION: heterosexual intercourse from the rear.

DOGS: 1. the tumblers on a safe. 2. (US) shoes.

DOG'S COCK: a sausage.

DOING THE PARTY: the stage of a three-card trick when one of the team pretends to be a winning player and so encourages mugs to bet.

DOLLYING: (Aus) brutal police questioning. Crushing or breaking quartz was known as dollying.

DONG: the penis.

DONNAH: 1. the Queen of Spades in the three-card trick, 'Find the Lady'. 2. an attractive woman or girlfriend, 'Never introduce your donnah to a pal.'

DOOGEE: heroin.

DO ONE'S LOT: to lose all one's money by gambling.

DOORMAN: the member of a robbery team whose duty it is to guard the door.

DO-RAG: (US street) a tight head scarf.

DOSE: 1. gonorrhoea. 2. a four-month sentence. 3. medication.

DOSH: 1. money 2. a tip or bribe, ex W. African.

DOSSER: 1. a tramp or one who sleeps rough, ex 18c doss = bed. 2. a drug taker.

DO THE BUSINESS: 1. to kill. 2. to complete a crime successfully. 3. to bribe a police officer. 4. to have sex.

DOUBLE BOAT: an elderly person who is losing his or her faculties and is therefore vulnerable to crime. Orig Northern use.

DOUBLE CARPET: 1. Six months' imprisonment. 2. the odds of 33-1 on a horse or dog.

DOUBLE-DECKER COFFIN: a coffin with an additional false bottom. The victim of a gangland killing is placed underneath the person whose family has paid for the funeral. A South London funeral home was alleged to have specialised in these double-decker burials and cremations in the 1960s and 1970s.

DOUBLE IN THE BUBBLE: a call at craps indicating that certain numbers circled on the table will pay odds of 2-1.

DOUBLE SAWBUCK: (Can) Ten years' imprisonment.

DOUBLE THE MELT: to have two orgasms before withdrawing the penis.

DOUCHE BAG: 1. A worthless person. 2. (US pris) a woman who has sexual relations with many other female prisoners.

DOWNERS: barbiturates.

DOWNHILL: the last half of a prison sentence.

DRAGGING: stealing from the backs of carts or lorries.

DRAGON, TO CHASE THE: to take heroin.

DRAW: cannabis.

DRECK: 1. an unpleasant man. 2. something poorly or shoddily made, ex Yiddish, literally shit.

DREYKOP: fraudsman or confidence trickster, literally twisted head.

DRINK; a bribe or money payment of unspecified amount but generally relatively small, particularly when used in mitigation, 'There was only a drink in it for me.'

DRINK OUT OF THE SAME BOTTLE; to be close friends.

DRIVE-BY; (US) a random shooting from a car.

DROP; 1. a place where messages can be left. 2. (US) a place where receipts are left by numbers runners. 3. the delivery of ransom money, 'You're to make the drop by the bridge.'

DROP GUN; see throwdown.

DROP MAN; (US) a man who collects receipts from a numbers runner.

DROPPER; a passer of worthless cheques.

DROPSY; a bribe or corrupt payment to the police.

DROWNED; a heavy loser at cards or dice. 'I'm drowned.'

DROWNING; obtaining entry to the home of an elderly person by pretending to be from the water board.

DRUM; 1. (Can) a cell. 2. home or flat. 'I've just spun golly's drum.' 3. (Aus) a brothel.

DRUM, THE; (Aus) reliable information, cf. the office.

DRUMMER; a clerk in a solicitor's office who is able to attract clients, ex US travelling salesman.

DRUMMING; 1. obtaining work for a firm of solicitors which specialises in criminal work. A clerk who is able to do this by drinking with criminals or placing money amongst police officers is highly prized. 2. breaking into property after first ringing the bell to discover whether anyone is at home.

DRY BATH; a complete cell and prisoner search which will include a rectal examination.

DUBBED UP; (Scots) to be locked up or in prison.

DUCK AND DIVE; to make a scratchy but not necessarily an honest living. 'How have you been?' ' I've been ducking and diving.'

DUCKS; the police, ducks and geese = police.

DUDE; a smartly dressed man, ex one who wears duds.

DUFF; 1. useless or fake. 2. a prison pudding which could be exchanged for cigarettes, see Frank Fraser, *Mad Frank's Diary*.

DUFF-UP; to beat up.

DUKES; fists, ex Duke of Yorks = forks = fingers.

DUMBBELL; a slide-hammer used for ripping out ignitions when stealing cars.

DUMMY; a deaf and dumb person.

DUMMY, TO BEAT THE; masturbation.

DUMMY RUN; a practice run.

DUMMY UP; to keep silent during police questioning.

DUN; to pursue a debt, ex the credit agency Dun and Bradstreet.

DUNNY; (Aus) an outside lavatory, poss. ex donniker.

DUNS; bailiffs.

DUSTED; 1. dead. 2. high on Angel Dust.

DUTCH ACT; suicide.

DUTCHMAN, THE; (Aus) a confidence trick when a sailor pretends he has missed his ship and needs money to catch up at the next port.

DUTCH TREAT; venereal disease.

DWELL THE BOX; to stay somewhere longer than necessary.

DYNAMITE; any narcotic of high potency.

E

E: Ecstasy; mixture of cocaine and LSD, a stimulant drug said to loosen sexual inhibitions and enhance sexual performance. It has been the cause of death in a number of cases of young women who have taken it in nightclubs where it is the drug of choice. The trade is enormous.

EAGLE: (US) 1. a winning player in a card game. 2. a criminal who works on his own.

EAR: a bent corner used to mark a card. In the three-card trick the dealer will be seen apparently deliberately bending a corner so signalling to the punter that it is the card on which to bet. The punter is mistaken.

EARN: to obtain money in a more or less dishonest fashion.

EARNER: a payment for work done or an opportunity to make a dishonest and unspecified profit, 'He's on an earner.' In financial terms an earner is worth more than a drink.

EASY RIDER: (Bl) a pimp, particularly a good one. W.C. Handy, 'Easy Rider, see what you have done.'

EAT: to perform fellatio or cunnilingus.

EAT PUSSY: to perform cunnilingus.

EDGE: 1. an advantage. 2. (Scots) a look-out, 'He's keeping the edge up.'

EGGS IN THE COFFEE: (US) something easy, a piece of cake.

EGG, TO BREAK AN: (US) to kill.

EIGHT BALL: 1. an African-American, ex the colour of the eight ball in Pool. 2. (US gang) to drink Old English 800 Malt Liquor.

EIGHTH: the quantity in which drugs were sold at street level, 'He sold me an eighth for £10.'

EIGHTY-SIX; 1. (US) to kill. 2. A child molester in for a crime so horrific that he is deemed a double 43, the former rule under which such prisoners could apply to be segregated from the remainder of the prison. The number of the rule has now been changed to R. 49.2 but 98.4 has yet to take over.

ELBOW; 1. (US) a police officer. 2. Part of a pickpocketing team, the elbow is the one who distracts the victim.

ELBOW, TO BE ON THE; scrounging. 'He's been on the elbow since the day he was born.'

ELEPHANT; 1. the anus, ex Elephant and Castle = arsehole. 2. drunk, elephant's trunk = drunk.

ELIMINATE; 1. to kill. 2. (euph) to pass bodily waste.

EME; the prison gang known as the Mexican Mafia, said to have been formed in San Quentin by a one-legged Irish prisoner.

EMPTY SUIT; a person who wishes to associate with mob members but has nothing to offer in return.

ENAMEL; (US) skin.

END; 1. a share of proceeds. 2. sexual intercourse, 'Are you having your end away?' 3. the worst. 4. the best, an example of value reversal.

ENDLESS BELT; (Aus) prostitute.

ENFORCER; 1. a debt collector. 2. a hard man. 3. a sledgehammer, particularly one used by the Flying Squad to effect an entry.

ENVELOPE; (US) a cash payment, usually a bribe or protection money.

EPSOM SALTS; Maltese, Epsom Salts = Malts.

EQUALISE; to kill.

EQUALISER; a gun.

ERASE; to murder.

EVIL ONE, THE; crystal methamphetamine, because of its extreme addictiveness.

EXES; 1. a six-month prison sentence, an example of slightly misspelled backslang. 2. £6. 3. expenses, such as payment for a stolen car, to be incurred in an enterprise, 'The job will have exes.' Now Standard English use by corporate executives.

EXPERIENCE; an LSD or mescaline experience.

EXPLORERS CLUB; (US) a group of LSD users.

EXTRAS; the additional and this time sexual services provided at a massage parlour or sauna.

EYE; a detective, ex the symbol of the Pinkerton Detective Agency, an open eye.

EYEBALL; to stare.

EYE-WASH; (US) tear gas.

F

F: (US) $50, ex the face of President Franklin on the bill.

F.A.: (euph) fuck all, i.e. nothing. In *Bring on the Empty Horses*, David Niven tells the story of the film director Michael Curtiz whose English was at best fractured. In a temper he said 'You say I know fuck nothing. You are wrong. I know fuck everything – I know fuck all.'

FACE: a known criminal. Before the formation of the Crown Prosecution Service it was regarded as good training for a young officer to go to a magistrates' court to listen to a bail hearing and see, in the public gallery, the faces or associates of the defendant who turned out to lend moral support.

FACTORY: 1. a police station specifically one of severe appearance such as the old Commercial Street nick; 2. a place where drugs are diluted, manufactured and packaged.

FADE: 1. the roll of dice. 2. to disappear quietly on the unexpected arrival of the police. 3. the loss of position by a horse in the closing stages of a race.

FAG: 1. a cigarette. 2. a male homosexual. There are a number of suggestions of the derivation, poss. ex World War One when smoking a cigarette rather than a pipe was regarded as effete. 3. the use of first year boys in British public schools as fags or servants and possibly to provide sexual favours to their masters. 4. a pickpocket, poss. ex Fagin in *Oliver Twist*.

FAG-HAG: (US) a woman who favours the company of male homosexuals.

FAIRY: a male homosexual.

FAIRY LADY: the feminine half of a lesbian relationship.

FALCONER: a confidence trickster posing as an aristocrat. Criminal history is littered with falconers including Gerald Chapman, 'The Count of

Gramercy Park' and Annie Gleason, who for some years masqueraded as the daughter of General Ulysses S. Grant.

FALL: an arrest, ex wrestling.

FALL GUY: a person designated by others to be arrested for a crime which he may or may not have committed.

FALL MONEY: cash set aside to pay for the services of a lawyer in the event of an arrest.

FAMILY JEWELS: the testicles.

FAN: to undertake a quick body search for concealed weapons.

FANNING: pickpocketing.

FANNY: 1. (UK) the vagina. 2. (US) the backside, 'He fell flat on his fanny.' A bag worn round the waist is in English slang a bum bag and not as in American a fanny bag. 3. nonsense or lies, 'Don't try that fanny with me.'

FANNY ADAMS: (often Sweet Fanny Adams) 1. euph. for fuck all. 2. (Navy) a cylindrical mess tin holding about a gallon.

Introduced in the 1860s, it originally contained tinned meat and was not popular. Shortly after its introduction a solicitor's clerk murdered and dismembered a young girl, Fanny Adams, near Alton, Hampshire. The standing joke was that the tin contained the remains of the child.

FAN POT: a liar or fanny merchant.

FART, BARF AND ITCH: (US) the FBI.

FARTLEBERRIES: pellets of faeces which cling to the hairs of the anus. In the 1960s a folk band toured under the name.

FART SACK: (US) a prison bed.

FAT: 1. (US) having a good supply of narcotics. 2. (Aus) an erection.

FAT BAGS: crack cocaine.

FAT CITY, TO BE IN: 1. (US) to be in the money. 2. a splendid state of affairs. The term can also be used derisorily.

FAT LADY SINGS, IT'S NOT

OVER UNTIL THE: defeat is not inevitable and there is still time for something to happen. A phrase now regarded as hopelessly politically incorrect and to be substituted by the baseball player Lou Gherig's 'It's not over until it's over.'

FAT MAN: (US BI) the electric chair.

FAT NUTS: (US pris) a man who steals by force or intimidates other prisoners is said to have Fat Nuts.

FATTY: a marijuana cigarette.

FAW: a gypsy. A Scottish clan of gypsies had the surname Faa. The word is extant in the North of England.

FEATHERS: female pubic hair. In the celebrated Australian Gun Alley case in which Colin Campbell Ross was convicted of killing a young girl, part of the evidence was that he was said to like girls before they 'grew feathers'.

FEEL, TO COP A: to touch a woman's sexual parts with or without her consent.

FEELER: a gentle inquiry, often undertaken by a lawyer, to see if arrangements can be made with the police over bail or other matters, 'Could you put the feelers out and see if I'm wanted?'

FENCE: a receiver of stolen property.

FERRET, TO EXERCISE THE: (Aus) to have sexual intercourse.

FERRY: (Aus) a prostitute. She carries many men.

FIBBIES: (US) the FBI.

FIELD MAN: (US) one who supervises a group of numbers runners.

FIELD MARSHAL: (US) a gang member who organises gang fights or other activities and may recruit members.

FIFI: an artificial vagina used for masturbation.

FIFTEEN ROUND BOUT: a long sex session. For safety reasons all title bouts are now boxed over twelve rounds.

FIFTH ESTATE: (US) the Syndicate or Mob.

FILA: (Sp pris) a knife.

FILE: 1. a pickpocket. 2. a criminal case, 'Is there a file on him?'

FILEASO: (Sp pris) a knife fight.

FILERO: (Sp pris) a knife or shank.

FILLET: (Aus) to dishonestly lose part of the prosecution evidence.

FILTER: to desert.

FILTH: (Scots) the police.

FIN: 1. $5. 2. (Can) a five-year sentence.

FIND THE LADY: the three-card trick.

FINEST: the police. A sarcastic term, 'London (or New York)'s finest haven't found the man.'

FINGER: to point out or give information, often to the police, naming names.

FINGER AND THUMB: the anus, ex finger and thumb = bum.

FINGER PIE: the manual stimulation of the clitoris.

FINGER WAVE: examination for drugs in the anus.

FINISHING SCHOOL: Borstal or more rarely a women's prison.

FINK: 1. an untrustworthy or unpleasant person, particularly a strike breaker. 2. a police informer, ex the dislike amongst criminals of the Pinkerton Detective Agency who liked to be called Pinks and which hired out men for strike breaking. See also Rat fink.

FIREPROOFER: (US) a confidence trickster specialising in preying on the religious, ex Hell fire.

FIRM: a gang. Ronnie and Reggie Kray ran The Firm and in the 1960s some members of the Flying Squad were described as being a 'firm within a firm'.

FIRMING: a gang beating-up.

FIRST BIRD: the first time in prison.

FISH: a new prison inmate. The period during which a prisoner would be referred to as a fish would last between three and six months.

FIST FUCK: to insert the hand and wrist into the vagina or anus. Particularly common amongst homosexuals attracted to sado-masochism, the practice can cause severe internal injuries.

FISTINA: masturbation. George Pelicanos, *Right as Rain*, 'He's been faithful to a girl Fistina for the last twenty years.' 'They say that'll make you blind too.'

FIT: (US) a home-made contrivance used to inject drugs.

FITTED: badly beaten, 'I fitted him', abb. 'I fitted him for his coffin.'

FIT UP: to plant or give false evidence to endeavour to ensure a conviction.

FIVE FINGER DISCOUNT: shoplifting.

FIVE-O: (US) the police, ex the television series *Hawaii Five-O*.

FIX, THE: the pre-ordained outcome of a sporting event or criminal trial, 'The fix is in.'

FIX, TO: 1. to arrange by bribery or threats. 2. to inject a drug.

FIZZER: (Aus) an informer.

FIZZGIG: (Aus) an informer.

FLADGE AND PADGE: flagellation and pageantry. Bondage and costume wearing for the purposes of sexual stimulation.

FLAG: (US Pris) to indicate a preference for homosexuality.

FLAKE OUT: to go to sleep, ex the method of feeding out a rope, laying it flat in long form.

FLAKING: the police practice of planting narcotics.

FLANNELFOOT: a housebreaker. The word was probably coined by the writer Edgar Wallace.

FLAP MAN: (Aus) one who passes bad cheques.

FLAPPING TRACK: an unlicensed greyhound track. In theory dogs which have run at such a track may not run at a licensed track so the dogs are often run under assumed names and, in practice, there is a steady two-way trade. Sometimes this is used as a form of training but more for betting purposes. In other cases the dogs may have been warned off licensed tracks for fighting.

FLASH, THE: the effect of cocaine and, to a lesser extent, methedrine.

FLASHER: a man who exposes his penis to women often quickly opening a coat or macintosh to do so. In extreme cases the man will have what appears to be the legs of trousers sewn to his coat.

FLATBACKER: a part-time prostitute.

FLATFOOT: a policeman, particularly a uniformed one.

FLEA: (Aus) a prisoner who is on good terms with both guards and other inmates. He hops from one to the other.

FLIM: 1. £5. 2. a five-year sentence.

FLIM-FLAM: to cheat or swindle.

FLIM-FLAM MAN: a conman.

FLIP FLOP: (US) a homosexual who will both pitch and catch (qv). It indicates a weakness on the part of the dominant partner.

FLIPWRECK: (Aus) a victim of chronic masturbation.

FLOATER: 1. a drowned person. 2. (Aus) a meat pie in pea soup, a cultural delicacy.

FLOG: to sell.

FLOG ONE'S MEAT: to masturbate.

FLOG THE LOG: to masturbate.

FLOP: (US) the time a parole board allocates before the next hearing.

FLOPHOUSE: a transient's hotel, often where the men sleep in dormitories.

FLOSS: to show off.

FLOWERY: prison, ex flowery dell = cell. The origin is in an old song, *Peter Bell*.

FLUFF: feminine lesbianism.

FLUFFER: a woman or man employed to maintain the interest of the male star between takes in a pornographic film. Michael Connolly, *Concrete Blonde*.

FLUSHING: drawing blood back into the syringe when taking drugs.

FLYING LESSON: the act of throwing oneself or another inmate from a prison landing.

FLYING YOUR COLOURS: to wear a gang's colours.

FLY THE FLAG: to be menstruating.

FOLD, TO: to give up suddenly as in cards 'I only drew a pair and I folded', or in a boxing match, this time often by arrangement, 'He'll fold in the third.'

FOLDING STUFF: paper money as opposed to coins, 'The only sure way to double your money is to fold it in your pocket.'

FOLLIES: Quarter Sessions, which until 1967 were held for serious but not indictable only crimes throughout England and Wales on a quarterly basis. The term is not used for the crown court which sits continuously.

FOOT SOLDIER: the lowest-ranking member of a criminal organisation.

FORK: the hand, Duke of Yorks = forks = fingers.

FORM: criminal convictions.

FOUR FIVE: a .45 calibre automatic pistol.

FOX: (Bl and m/cycle) a woman.

FOXY: sexy, ex fox.

FRAME, TO: to obtain a conviction by false evidence.

FRAME, TO BE IN THE; 1. to be suspected of a criminal offence. 2. to be left money in a will, ex the practice of putting the winning numbers in a horse race in a skeletal frame. 3. to be on call. In the 1960s Scotland Yard maintained a rota of senior detectives in a wooden frame which changed daily. An officer 'in the frame' could be sent to the provinces or abroad at an hour's notice.

FRANGER; (Aus) a condom.

FREE AIR; (US) released from prison.

FREEBIE; something obtained without payment, particularly a ticket or sex with a prostitute.

FREEHANDER; (US) an expert forger who does not need a lamp, dry pen etc.

FREE WORLD; the world outside prison.

FRENCH; oral sex.

FRESH FISH; new, and specifically a young, inmate in prison, one who is liable to be subject to sexual predations.

FRIDAY 13ᵀᴴ; Attica prison, New York State.

FRIEND OF OURS; see *amico nostro*.

FRIG; to have sex, euph. for fuck.

FRIGGING ABOUT; fooling about. Friggers are pieces of glass such as walking sticks or rolling pins made by 19c apprentices at England's Nailsea glassworks in their spare time.

FRIGHTENER; 1. A man employed to collect payment, often from recalcitrant book-makers; sometimes to persuade a witness to change his or her evidence. 2. (pl) threats generally, 'I put the frighteners on her.'

FRISK; 1. to search quickly for stolen goods, drugs or concealed weapons, ex the gambolling of a lamb. 2. (US) a pickpocket.

FROG; a girl with no morals. She will hop into bed with anyone.

FRONT; 1. a person in the public view shielding the real owner of a club or business, particularly a long firm fraud, from the police. Fronts rarely have criminal records which may make prosecution or conviction more difficult. 2. to confront a suspect with his or her identifier. Before the Police and Criminal Evidence Act 1984 which effectively banned the practice this was a popular way of dealing with a suspect who caused trouble about appearing on an identification parade. 3. to brazen things out.

FRONT THE GAFF; to go to the main door of a building with a view to committing burglary.

FROTTAGE; rubbing the penis against a woman in a crowded place.

FRUIT; a homosexual, 'Why is San Francisco like a Hershey Bar?' 'Because it's full of flakes, fruits and nuts.'

FRUITFLY; a straight woman who associates with homosexuals.

FRY; to be electrocuted in the electric chair.

FUCK; 1. to have sex. 2. to cheat or swindle, 'I fucked him over.'

FUCK ABOUT; to be a nuisance, 'Shut up and don't fuck about.'

FUCKING; very, used as an adjective to give emphasis, 'He's fucking crazy.'

FUCK OFF; to leave or disappear, 'I don't know where he's fucked off to.' 'You like sex, right? And you like travel, right? Now, fuck off.'

FUDGE PACKER; (Can) homosexual.

FUGAZI (FUGAZZI, FUGAZY); (US) fake, counterfeit.

FUGLY; extremely ugly, abb. fucking ugly.

FULL; full of drugs.

FULL HOUSE; to have either both head and body lice or both syphilis and gonorrhoea.

FUNNY FARM; a mental hospital.

FURBURGER, TO EAT A; to practice cunnilingus.

FUR-TRADER; a White slaver.

FUTURE; the testicles. A common graffito in a male public lavatory was 'The future of Britain is in your hands.'

FUZZ; police.

G

G: (US) 1. $1,000, ex the portrait of President Grant on the face of a note. 2. a gun, as in G-man. 3. £1,000 (never common).

G 27: a prison gang originally formed in Puerto Rico but which now has members in East Coast prison systems in America.

GABBER: a police officer, a corruption of gavver (qv).

GAFF: 1. a house or flat. 2. an aid to cheating at cards or dice. 3. any sort of swindle. In the world of the carnival the hierarchy depended on whether a gaff was required to deceive the punters. So, a Fat Lady who did not need to resort to a gaff would be top of the blow-off (qv) and the Half Man-Half Woman would be in a less exalted position because of the need to resort to gaffs such as depilatories, over exercise of one half of the body or a false breast. 4. a mistake.

GAFFLE UP: (US) to arrest a gang member.

GAG: to silence, ex the 17c torture of filling the mouth with iron pins.

GA(U)GE: (US gang) a shotgun.

GAGGER: (US) a cigar, ex a gag in the mouth.

GALBOY: the female partner in a homosexual relationship.

GALLERY 13: (US) a prison graveyard.

GALLINA: (Hisp pris) a coward, ex chicken.

GALLOUS: (Scots) flashy, hard, smart.

GAM: 1. fellatio or cunnilingus, ex Fr *gamaruche* or *gamahuche*, 'I was giving him a gam, sir.' 2. a leg, originally a spindly or deformed one, ex Fr *gamb(e)*.

GAME: 1. full of courage, particularly used in the prize ring where one boxer was known as The Game Chicken. 2. a willingness to expose oneself to ridicule, ex the play on words in TV shows such as *Game for a Laugh*. 3. open to bribery, 'Is he game?', ex 19c dishonest. 4. (US gang) criminal activity.

GAME. ON THE: engaged in prostitution.

GAME PULLET; a young prostitute.

GAMMY: injured or lame, ex gam.

GANDER: a quick or surreptitious look.

GANGBANG: 1. a multiple rape. 2. (US) a fight with a rival gang.

GANGBANGER: (US) a member of a street gang, particularly on the West Coast.

GANGBUSTER: a law officer who specifically seeks to break up organised crime. Bert Wickstead, *Gangbuster.*

GANG JACKET: (US) one who has been validated as a gang member, i.e. allowed to wear the jacket.

GANGLAND: the Underworld, specifically Chicago.

GANGSTER: 1. a career criminal who will use force. 2. (US) HIV, 'He's got the gangster.'

GANJA: marijuana.

GAPO: (US) extreme body odour, ex gorilla armpit odour.

GARRITY: insane, literally hopping mad, ex Freddy Garrity of Freddy and the Dreamers who performed an awkward dance, The Freddy.

GARTER: (US) an indeterminate sentence, one which may be lengthened or shortened.

GAS: to spray with C.S. gas.

GASH: 1. the mouth. 2. a prostitute. 3. a woman considered only in the sexual sense, 'Have you had any gash recently?' 4. (US) specifically a White woman, raped by an Afro-American. 5. rubbish.

GASHBIN: a dustbin.

GAS HOUSE: (US) the communal lavatory in a prison.

GAS METER BANDIT: derisory term for small-time thief.

GASSER: a suicide by inhaling fumes.

GASSING: 1. obtaining entry to the flats and houses of the elderly by pretending to be from the Gas Board. 2. (US) throwing fluid at a prison guard.

GAT: 1. (US) a gun, ex Gatling gun. 2. a shank for use in a prison fight.

GATE: the money collected from spectators at an event.

GATE ARREST: the immediate arrest for an outstanding offence of a prisoner as he leaves the jail. Unsurprisingly the procedure is not popular with prisoners who can often be persuaded by the police to have matters taken into consideration at the hearing of the first offence. This has many advantages to many people. The defendants get very little more in the way of prison by showing their repentance. The police clear up their books. Gate arrest has recently become common in New York where mobsters emerging

from lengthy sentences find themselves re-charged.

GATE FEVER: the emotion shown by prisoners nearing the end of their sentence.

GATEMOUTH: (Bl) a chronic gossip.

GAVVERS: police, ex Romany.

GAY BASHING: (US) beating of homosexuals.

G.B.H.: Grievous Bodily Harm, 'I gave him a spot of GBH.'

GEAR: 1. drugs. 2. clothing. The story is told of Sir Allan Green, former Director of Public Prosecutions, that as a young barrister prosecuting a motorcyclist he asked the man what gear he was in. 'Me usual, studs and leathers,' was the reply.

GEEK: a freak or now a nerdy (qv) person, ex carnival where to see the geek act cost extra money and, like the murals at Pompeii, would only be shown to men after the main tour. The geek, very often a fake, would appear to eat the heads off live chickens or snakes. This would be the subject of a gaff (qv) in itself as live chickens cost money. The term was said to have first been used of a man, Wagner, from West Virginia. The Tyrone Power film, *Sunshine Alley* features a geek act.

GEE-UP: a staged fight made to look real for the crowd.

GELT: money, ex Yiddish.

GEMMIE: (Scot) a hard man, enforcer.

GENERIC: a fake.

GEORGE: (Aus) menstruation.

GERT AND DAISY: the Kray Twins, ex the Cockney radio comediennes Ethel and Doris Walters.

GET: see *git*.

GET A PLACE READY: to find an inconspicuous grave.

GET DOWN: (US) fighting.

GET TO: to bribe a policeman, juror, greyhound trainer etc.

GET-UP: something fake or false, 'The arrest was a get-up.'

G.H.B.: the so-called date-rape drug.

GHETTO STAR: a neighbourhood celebrity, often a drug dealer.

GHOST: (US) 1. to disappear. 2. a lawyer who advises but does not appear in court. 3. (BI) a White person.

GHOSTING: the practice of transferring a troublesome prisoner to another establishment during the night and without warning. This can be done to break up trouble makers and also defeat inquiries into allegations of sexual assaults or beatings.

GHOST SQUAD: a team of undercover police officers set up after the Second World War to deal with highjackers and Black marketeers and effectively unaccountable for their time and methods. The Squad was disbanded in the early 1950s when it was felt that some officers were becoming too close to the criminals.

GHOST TOWN; the Bronx, New York.

GIGGLE; 1. (Aus) a bribe. In a recent corruption case in New South Wales a group of Sydney officers referred to themselves as The Gigglers. 2. the penis.

GIGGLE HOUSE; (Aus) a mental hospital.

GIGGLE JUICE; (Aus) intoxicating liquor.

GIMMIES; demanding with menaces.

GIN; (Aus) an aboriginal.

GIN AND JAGUAR BELT; smart districts of Surrey, England thought to be particularly suitable for burglaries.

GIN AND JAGUAR BIRD; married woman from above thought not to be averse to extra-marital intercourse.

GIN BURGLAR/JOCKEY; (Aus) a white man who has sex with an aboriginal woman.

GINGER; 1. a homosexual,

ginger beer = queer, 'Is he ginger?' 2. (Aus) a prostitute's client.

GIN-MILL; (US) saloon or bar.

GIN ON THE ROCKS; (Aus) sex with an Aboriginal woman.

GIT; a bastard, now a general term of abuse, poss. ex 'Is that one of his get (or offspring)?' Poss. ex stockbreeding for the offspring of a stray stallion that had mixed with a group of mares.

GIT-DOWN TIME; (Bl) the time of day when a prostitute begins work.

GIT GO; (Bl) the beginning.

GIVE A PASS; (US) to grant a reprieve.

GIVE A PERMANENT WAVE; (US) to die by electrocution.

GIVE HIM THE BIG PICTURE; (US gang) to kill.

GIVE HIM THE BUS TICKET HOME; (US gang) to kill.

GIVE IT A SPIN; 1. to attempt,

poss. ex a test drive of a car. 2. to search, 'We spun his drum.'

GIVE IT THE BIG ONE ('UN); 1. to boast or brag. 2. to intimidate.

GIVEN A LIFE, TO BE; release after a search by the police. There was often a price to pay in terms of money or information.

GIVE UP; the proportion of earnings to be handed to a superior, spec. Chicago use.

GIZZIT; a promotional free handout such as a CD or ballpoint pen, ex 'give us it'.

GLADIATOR SCHOOL; (US) a prison for young unruly inmates.

GLASGOW HELLO (KISS); a headbutt.

GLASS; the penis.

GLASS, TO BLOW HIS; fellatio.

GLASS HOUSE; army detention centres, ex the detention barracks at North Camp, Aldershot which had a glass roof.

GLASSING; to slash, specifically a face, with a broken bottle or glass.

GLASS JAW; a boxer unable to sustain a punch to the chin is said to have a glass jaw.

GLIM; a match or light.

GLORY, TO GET THE; used of a prisoner who has genuinely turned to religion or who purports to have done so to obtain preferential treatment or an early release.

G-MEN; the FBI. The word is said to have been coined by Machine Gun Kelly who, when FBI agents burst into his room to arrest him for the kidnapping of millionaire Charley Urschel in 1933, called out, 'Don't shoot G-men.' The term was taken up enthusiastically by J. Edgar Hoover, then head of the FBI, as good publicity.

GOAT THROTTLING; classic Mafia strangulation technique in which the victim's hands and feet are bound with a single cord or rope and passed through a noose around the neck. The more he struggled the tighter the noose became. In the case of Giuseppe Di Maggio, whose body was found in the Gulf of Palermo in the autumn of 2000, he was then put in a plastic bag and thrown in the sea.

GOBBLE; oral sex, particularly between males.

GOBBLEGOO; (US) a prostitute who prefers oral intercourse.

GOBBLERS' GULCH; an outdoor homosexual rendezvous. One such area was on Primrose Hill, Regents Park, London.

GO DOWN; 1. to be sentenced to a term of imprisonment, ex to go down the steps from the dock to the prison. 2. to participate in oral sex.

GOD'S GARBAGE; (Aus) a criminal biker.

GOFER; a lackey or underling, 'He will gofer this and gofer that.'

GO HOME; 1. to be released from prison. 2. to die.

GOING ON LINE; (US gang) joining a gang.

GOING OVER; a bad beating, 'I give him a real going over.'

GOLD AND SILVER; bi-sexual.

GOLDBERG; (US Bl) a neutral term for a Jewish person.

GOLDBRICKING; (US) malingering, ex the 1860s confidence trick in which the punter believes he is being sold a gold bar or lends money against such an object. A goldbricker is therefore a fraudsman.

GOLDEN MILKSHAKE; urination in the mouth.

GOLDEN SHOWER; the service offered by prostitutes of urinating on the client or allowing him or herself to be urinated upon.

GOLFER; (US) a Cadillac, ex caddy.

GON(N)ER; 1. a dying person. 2. a person marked for death.

GONIF(F); a small-time thief, ex Yiddish.

GONK; a prostitute's client.

GONSIL; (US) 1. a young thief. 2. a catamite. 3. an informer.

GOOD PEOPLE; a loyal member of the Underworld or one generally supportive of it, 'He's good people.'

GO OFF; (Aus) to be caught, to have something confiscated.

GOOD TIME; (Can) remission.

GOOF; 1. (Can) a term of abuse amongst prisoners. 2. to make a mistake.

GOOFBALLS; barbiturates.

GOOLIES; testicles, ex Hindi *goolies*, a round object.

GOOLIES, TO HAVE SOMEONE BY THE; to be in total control. A person whose testicles are being gripped is in no position to argue.

GOON SQUAD; (Can) prison riot squad.

GO OVER THE WALL; to escape from prison. J.P. Bean, *Over the Wall*.

GOPHER; a safe with an intricate time lock.

GOPHER-MOB; a team of bank tunnellers.

GO Q.E.; to give evidence for the prosecution against one's co-accused in return for a lighter sentence or, better still, immunity from prosecution, literally Queen's Evidence.

GORILLA; 1. (Aus) $1,000. 2. (US) a thug or enforcer, particularly one who would kill in times of difficulty.

GORILLA PIMP; (BI) a pimp who uses extreme violence to his string.

GOULASH; (US) misleading information.

GRAB; 1. to arrest. 2. to steal.

GRAB A LITTLE AIR; (US) to hold one's hands up, to surrender.

GRAFTER; 1. a pickpocket. 2. a general hardworker.

GRAND; £1000 or $1,000.

GRANNY; a legitimate business used as a cover, e.g. to dispose of stolen goods.

GRAPES; 1. haemorrhoids. 2. gossip, 'Give me the grapes on him.'

GRASS; an informer, poss. ex The Inkspots, *Whispering Grass*, grasshopper = shopper/copper. 2. cannabis.

GRASS EATER; a police officer who will accept bribes but will not actively pursue them.

GRASSHOPPER; police officer, ex grasshopper = copper.

GRASS, IN THE; on the run from the police.

GRAVY, TO DISH OUT THE; to hand out heavy sentences.

GRAY; (US) a White person, e.g. gray dude etc.

GREASE; a bribe. Grease facilitates the wheels turning.

GREEK; anal intercourse, ex the supposed proclivity of Greek males.

GREEN; money.

GREEN GOODS; counterfeit money.

GREEN GOODS GAME; a confidence trick in which the victim is left holding newspaper rather than the money he believes is there.

GREEN ICE; emeralds.

GREEN LIGHT; to be marked for death.

GREEN RUB; ill fortune, ex the green discharge produced when suffering from gonorrhoea.

GREENS; sexual intercourse, 'Are you getting your greens?'

G-RIDE; (US) a stolen vehicle.

GRIEF; inconvenience, 'All this is causing me a whole load of grief.'

GRIFTER; one who lives by his wits in criminal operations, e.g. a pickpocket, card sharp, swindler.

GRILL; to question.

GROIN; a diamond ring.

79

GROOVY; (Scot) a scar.

GROUND COVER; (Aus) a young woman.

GROUNDERS; (US) a homicide case which can be solved reasonable swiftly.

GROUTER; (Aus) an unfair advantage.

GRUB; (NZ) information.

GRUMBLE; sexual intercourse, grumble and grunt = cunt.

GRUNTER; (Aus) a young woman, used with sexual connotations.

GULLION; stolen jewellery.

GUNNED DOWN; to be the victim of the throwing of faeces or urine.

GUNNER; a prisoner who masturbates whilst in the presence of a female warder.

GUN RUN; (US) New York police term for a radio call to an incident involving firearms.

GUNS; hoodlums.

GUNSIL; see gonsil.

GUN, TO EAT ONE'S; (US pol) to commit suicide.

GUY, TO HAVE A; to walk away, Guy Fawkes = walks.

GUY THE COURSE; (Scot) to run away.

GYPSY CAB; an unlicensed New York taxi.

GYPSY WIRES; illegal wiretapping by the police or other Government agency.

H

H; heroin.

HABIT; a drug addition.

HACK; a prison guard.

HACK IT; to do something easily.

HAIRCUT; 1. a short prison sentence, ex the days when prisoners had to have short hair. 2. a motor car with miles trimmed from the odometer.

HAIR PIE; 1. the vagina. Charles Willeford, *Miami Blues,* 'What I fear is that little hair pie, that's what I fear.' 2. cunnilingus.

HAIRY; dangerous.

HAIRY-APE; rape.

HALF A BAR; Fifty pence.

HALF A MAN; (US pris) a homosexual.

HALF AND HALF; 1. a prostitute's service of half oral and half straight sex. 2. the service in a sauna where the client may massage the girl for half the time.

HALF ASSED WISEGUY; a person who seeks admission to the Mafia.

HALF A STRETCH; six months' imprisonment.

HALF A TON; £50.

HALF BRASS; a girl who will hand out sexual favours freely but does not necessarily accept money.

HALF INCH; to steal, half inch = pinch.

HALF IRON; a bisexual.

HALF OF MARGE; Police Sergeant, half of marge = serge.

HAM AND CHEESE SANDWICH; (US) a payoff to a union delegate.

HAMMERS; (US) the police, hammers and saws = laws.

HAMPTON; the penis, Hampton

Wick = prick. Used usually as a term of derision, 'He's a right Hampton.'

HANDBOOK; (US) an employee or financial backer of a book-maker.

HANDFUL; 1. £5. 2. a five-year prison sentence. 3. (Racing) five lengths.

HAND JOB; masturbation, often by another party as in a massage parlour. It was argued unsuccessfully that this did not legally constitute prostitution.

HANDLE; 1. a title. 2. to be a skilled boxer, now more generally to conduct oneself well in difficult circumstances, 'Can he handle it?'

HAND MUCKER; a card palmer.

HAND SHANDY; masturbation.

HANDS UP, TO PUT ONE'S; 1. to confess. 2. to plead guilty.

HANGER HOOKS; hooks sewn into the lining of clothing worn by professional shoplifters.

HANGING JUDGE; one who will favour the prosecution and then impose a severe sentence. Henry Hawkins, the Victorian judge, was known as Hanging Hawkins. A more modern example would be Mr Justice Melford Stevenson who presided over the first Kray trial.

HANG IT ON THE LIMB; (US) to escape from prison.

HANG PAPER; (US) to pass worthless cheques.

HANS CHRISTIAN ANDERSEN; a police officer who invents verbals (qv) and is therefore a story teller, 'He's a right Hans Christian Andersen.'

HAPPY BAG; the bag used to conceal shotguns before a bank robbery.

HAPPY DUST; cocaine.

HARD; chewing tobacco.

HARD MACK; a pimp who uses violence, see mack.

HARD ON; to have an erection.

HARD ON, TO HAVE A H.O. FOR SOMEONE; 1. to dislike them. 2. to be sexually excited by them.

HARD ROCK; 1. a gambler who refuses to lend money. 2. a difficult player to beat.

HARDWARE; weapons or firearms.

HARD WAY; 1. a sentence served without remission. Most of the sentences imposed on Mad Frank Fraser were served the hard way following fights with prison officers and attacks on governors. Part of the evidence against James Hanratty, hanged for the A6 murder, was that the killer had said he had done his Borstal the hard way as had Hanratty. 2. (US) death by violence.

HARDWAY BET; the numbers 4, 6, 8 and 10 which are achieved by a throw of the dice resulting in two twos, threes etc. The call is more difficult than 1 and 3, 2 and 4 etc.

HARD YACKER; (Aus) hard work, ex yackers, hard wearing canvas workman's trousers at the turn of the 19c.

HARLEM SUNSET; (US) a fatal knife wound.

HAROLD; celluloid, a favourite tool of burglars, ex the silent film star Harold Lloyd.

HARP; 1. a harmonica. 2. an Irish immigrant to America.

HASH; hashish.

HAT; (US) $25, a bribe or gratuity given to a police officer for information.

HATCHET MAN; hired killer, ex the use of the hatchet by the Tong gangs of early 20c.

HATE FACTORY, THE; HMP Wandsworth, ex the alleged brutality of some warders over the years.

HATER; (US gang) an informer.

HAUL ASS; to leave in a hurry.

HAVE A WORD WITH SOMEONE; to beat up.

HAVE IT; 1. to accept the truth of an accusation and so 2. to plead guilty.

HAVE IT AWAY; 1. to complete a crime successfully. 2. to escape from the police. 3. to have sexual intercourse.

HAVE IT OFF; as have it away.

HAVE IT ON ONE'S TOES; to escape from the police.

HAVE ONE'S COLLAR FELT; to be arrested.

HAVE SOMEONE OVER; 1. to outwit. 2. to seduce.

HAWK; an expert at identifying police officers. It is his duty to warn the stickman (qv) in a carnival of the presence of the law to enable him to disconnect any cheating devices.

HAWKSHAW; (WI) the police, ex 19c.

HAW MAWS; (Scot) Haw baws = ba's = testicles.

HBI; housebreaking instruments.

HEAD; (US) a victim.

HEADBANGER; a mentally disturbed prisoner, ex banging one's head against a wall.

HEAD COLD; (US) gonorrhea.

HEADHUNTER; a contract killer.

HEADS; a warning shout.

HEAD, TO GIVE; to fellate.

HEAP; an old motor vehicle.

HEAP CLOUTING; stealing motor vehicles.

HEARTS; penniless, Hearts of Oak = broke.

HEAT; (US) pressure, particularly unwanted pressure from the police.

HEATER; (US) a gun particularly a revolver.

HEAVEN; the date-rape drug GHB.

HEAVY; 1. a major and often violent criminal. 2. a member of the Flying Squad, usually used in the plural.

haywire: badly awry

HEAVY BIT; (US) a long prison sentence.

HEAVY MOB; 1. Flying, Robbery or Serious Crime Squads. 2. a group of warders in prison standing by to deal with trouble.

HEAVY TIME; 1. a long prison sentence 2. crimes of violence 'I'm wrapping up (quitting) heavy time.'

HEAVY WORK; armed robbery.

HEDGE; 1. the crowd around a street salesman or three-card trick game. 2. to lay off a bet so that whatever the result a gain is more likely.

HEEL; 1. a sneak thief. 2. to avoid payment of a hotel bill. 3. to use rough tactics, so 4. the villain in a professional wrestling match.

HEELED; 1. rich as in well heeled. 2. (US) to be in possession of a dangerous weapon, usually a gun.

HEELER; a bouncer.

HEIST; a robbery, often high-jacking, ex hoist.

HEIST IN THE PRATT; (US) a kick or more usually a knee in the buttocks.

HELLO; a standard salutation in a letter from prison, 'Give Sis a big hello.'

HEN; Glaswegian term of endearment.

HEN PEN; a women's prison.

HERB; a weak prison inmate.

HIDE; (US) 1. a wallet or purse. 2. a prostitute. 3. a passive homo-sexual.

HIDE, A PIECE OF; sexual intercourse.

HIDE THE SALAMI; (US) sexual intercourse.

HIGHJACK; to commit a robbery, usually of a lorry which is then dumped. One version of the origin comes from the tendency of Americans to call a stranger Jack. In the days of Prohibition a robber stealing a lorry of liquor would tell the driver to raise his arms saying, 'High, Jack'. Another version is that since jack was mining slang for zinc the word comes from a theft of that metal.

HIGH OFF THE HOG, TO LIVE: living well, ex the best cut of pork.

HIGH ROLLER: a heavy gambler.

HIGH SIDE: to show off.

HINIE: 1. hideout/highway; 2. (US pris) the anus.

HIPE: see hype.

HIT: 1. to kill 2. to draw another card, 'Hit me.' 3. to make a quick profit at cards or dice. 4. to draw a winning number in a lottery. 5. to dilute drugs prior to selling them. 6. to obtain drugs. 7. to borrow money. 8. a kiss, ex hit and miss = kiss. 9. to get drunk, ex hit and missed = pissed.

HIT IN THE NECK: (US) to have no chance, ex a stab in the neck which would usually prove fatal.

HIT MAN: a contract killer.

HITMOBILE: a car, traditionally a black sedan, specifically used for a contract killing. Felix 'Milwaukee Phil' Alderisio had a car with hidden gun compartments, reinforced panels on the sides, extra shocks, bullet-proof windows and revolving licence plates.

HIT ON: (BI) 1. to attempt to make a score of drugs or money. 2. to attempt to add a woman to a pimp's stable.

HITS: a pair of crooked dice which will not combine to make the number seven.

HIT THE BOARDS: an instruction to a dice player to ensure that the dice hit the far end of the table and bounce back.

HIT THE BRICKS: 1. to go outdoors and specifically 2. to be released from prison.

HIT THE TOE: (Aus) to abscond.

HOBBIT: a prisoner who complies with or, worse, sucks up to the system.

HOBBIT HOLE: somewhere the hobbits go, e.g. the television room in prison.

HOG: (US) 1. a motor car, esp. a Cadillac, 'It is a hog for gasoline.' 2. a prisoner who will not back down.

HOGMAN: see Bellman.

HOIST: to steal, particularly as a shoplifter. In 19c it was to get into property through open windows. An accomplice gave the man a hoist up.

HOLE: 1. the vagina. 2. the anus. 3. a passive homosexual prisoner who does not belong to a particular person. 4. (US) solitary confinement cell.

HOLE, TO GO IN THE: to fall off scaffolding.

HOLLOW TOOTH: New Scotland Yard, an ironic term used by officers and criminals alike.

HOME AND COLONIAL: the London-based Regional Crime Squad. The squad had both Metropolitan (Home) and provincial (Colonial) officers and the name derives from a now defunct chain of grocery shops.

HOME BOY (HOMEY): a fellow gang member from the same neighbourhood.

HOME INVASION: a mass robbery at a dwelling usually in which the occupants are beaten.

HONEYMAN: a prison lavatory cleaner.

HONEY POT: a lavatory.

HONKY: 1. (Bl) term of abuse for a White person. 2. a factoryhand.

HOOCH: illicit liquor, ex Native American *hoocheno*.

HOOD: a male criminal engaged in professional crime, poss. ex hoodlum which itself may derive from the Hoodler brothers of San Francisco in the 1860s, or the mugger's practice of turning up a collar to make identification more difficult.

HOOF: 1. a homosexual, iron hoof = poof. 2. (US) to hide smuggled goods in the rectum.

HOOK: 1. a thief, ex hooks = fingers. 2. a bent pin used to inject narcotics.

HOOKER: 1. a prostitute, ex the Hook a red-light district of the Bronx, NY or the Civil War General Hooker who encouraged prostitutes to follow his soldiers or the Dutch *hoeker* = huckster. 2. (US) an outstanding warrant. 3. a glass.

HOON: (Aus) a procurer of prostitutes but now general insult, poss. ex the German.

HOOP: to hide goods in the rectum.

HOOSEGOW: (US) 1. a prison. 2. a lavatory, ex Span *husgado*.

HOP: 1. a sleight of hand which, made after a cut of a pack of cards, replaces them in their original position. 2. opium.

HOP-HEAD: 1. a drug addict. 2. an ignorant person or fool.

HORSE: 1. heroin, poss. ex an old brand name, White Horse, poss. ex the association with doping horses. It may also be that it had more kick than other drugs. 2. $1,000, ex circus use, ex a G or a Gee-Gee. 3. a homosexual, ex horse's hoof = poof. 4. a prostitute or a short-term girlfriend. 5. gonorrhea, ex horse and trap = clap. 6. a prison officer who will smuggle letters and other goods on behalf of prisoners.

HORSESHIT: rubbish.

HORSE TO HORSE: (US) everything being equal.

HOSE JOB: oral sex.

HOTEL: 1. a police station as opposed to prison. 2. HMP Strangeways, Manchester.

HOT-LOT: the Flying Squad or the Special Patrol Group.

HOTPLATE HAMSTER: a prison officer who eats the prisoners' food.

HOT RAIL: the practice in American prisons of a group of inmates standing around a prisoner and his visitor so they may have sex.

HOTWIRE; to start a motorcar without a key by short circuiting ignition wires.

HOUSE; 1. to trace a person's home or residence. 2. to find stolen property. 3. a brothel. Polly Adler, *A House is not a Home*.

HOUSE OF MANY SLAMMERS; prison.

HUFFLE; see bagpipe.

HUMP; to have sexual intercourse.

HUMP; to have the; to be annoyed.

HUMPTY; sexual intercourse.

HURRY-UP, DONE ON THE; action taken without adequate preparation, sometimes given as an explanation for failure, 'We had to do it on the hurry-up.'

HURT; 1. (BI) to have financial difficulties. 2. to be in need of drugs.

HUSSY; a woman of easy virtue, ex housewife.

HUSTLE; 1. orig, to commit a robbery. 2. to obtain dishonestly. 3. to obtain a bet by falsely making the odds look attractive to the punter, eg purposely playing cards, snooker or pool badly until the stakes and odds are raised. 4. to practise prostitution.

HUSTLER; 1. a con man. 2. a male prostitute.

HYNA; (Hisp) a girlfriend.

HYPE; (US) 1. a short change trick in which the con man counts out money in front of his victim in such a way as to persuade him not to bother to count it himself. Coins have, however, been palmed. 2. to talk up a situation, e.g. a boxing match. 3. to cheat. 4. to lay the groundwork for a scam; to build up a potential victim for the kill. In all cases the victim is effectively hypnotised. 5. a hypodermic needle.

I

ICE: 1. diamonds in particular and, by extension, jewellery. 2. protection money paid to a police officer to allow an illegal drinking or gambling club to remain open. It takes the heat off. 3. any extra payment to obtain a benefit. 4. (US) anything valueless. 5. to kill.

ICEBOX, TO BE IN THE: solitary confinement in prison.

ICECREAM: a narcotic.

ICE CUBE: crack cocaine.

ICEMAN: (US) 1. a professional killer and therefore, in the abstract, death. Eugene O'Neill, *The Iceman Cometh*. 2. a person who distributes protection money. 3. a jewel thief. 4. an official who makes worthless promises. 5. a coolheaded gambler.

I.D.B.: illicit diamond buying.

I.D., TO: to identify or pick out, possibly on a parade where witnesses are asked to identify a suspect from a line up of eight or more people.

IFFY: 1. a risky undertaking, 'It's a bit iffy.' 2. stolen or dishonestly obtained goods, 'They're a bit iffy.' 3. a doubtful or dishonest person, 'My brief's a bit iffy.'

IF MONEY: if things turn out well.

IKEY: a Jewish person, ex Ikey Mo, ex Isaac Moses.

ILLEGAL GARDENING: cultivating cannabis and in particular skunk weed.

ILLYWHACKER: (Aus) a confidence trickster, generally a smalltime one who often operated at country fairs.

IN AND OUT MAN: an opportunist thief.

IN BACK: the death cell.

INCA: the highest-ranking officer in the Latin Kings street gang.

IN DUTCH: in trouble.

IN HOCK: in pawn or debt.

INK: (US) a tattoo.

INKSLINGER: a prisoner who draws tattoos.

IN MY MOUTH: (Bl) someone who is listening to a conversation, 'He's in my mouth.'

INSIDE: in prison.

INSIDE JOB: a robbery or theft which can only have taken place with the co-operation of the owner (for insurance purposes) or the staff.

IN SPADES: doubly sure, ex the highest-ranking suit in a pack of cards.

IN STIR: in prison.

IN STOOK: in difficulties, ex Yiddish.

INTERNATIONAL GAS METER BANDIT: derisory term for a small-time or unsuccessful thief.

IN, THE: 1. an entrée. 2. influence generally. 3. (Scot) to have a contact in a place to be robbed.

IN THE CAR: to be in a tight circle of friends.

IN THE CLOUDS: high on drugs.

IN THE HAT: marked for death, ex the drawing of lots from a hat. The one with the marked piece of paper had to kill the target. In theory only the person who drew the paper should know who was the killer.

IN THE MIX: involved in gang activity.

IRISH WAY: heterosexual anal intercourse, used to prevent pregnancy and avoid the sin of *coitus interruptus*. A criminal offence until 1994.

IRON: 1. a homosexual, iron hoof = poof, originally specifically a male prostitute. 2. a gun. 3. (US) a motor car. 4. money.

IRON MAN: (US) 1. $1. 2. a tireless athlete.

IRON OUT: 1. to solve a prob-

in the bag

lem, ex the use of the iron to take out wrinkles. 2. to launder money. 3. to kill.

IRONS: (US) 1. knuckledusters. 2. handcuffs.

ISLAND, THE: the Isle of Wight, specifically HMP Parkhurst. Because of the surrounding currents and the ease of sealing off the ferries, to escape from the Island itself is regarded as almost impossible.

ITALIAN FOOTBALL: a bomb.

ITALIAN NECKTIE: (US) a method of strangulation when a length of rope is wrapped around the victim's neck and each end is pulled by a killer.

IT LOOKS LIKE RAIN: an arrest is imminent.

IVORIES: 1. teeth, ex boxing. 2. piano keys. 3. dice. 4. billiard balls. All because of their composition.

J

JACK: (UK) 1. an erection, ex ejaculate. 2. a policeman or detective. The usage is common in the North of England and often refers to junior officers. In Liverpool at the time of the murder of Julia Wallace in 1920 the police were ironically known as Springheeled Jacks from the speed with which they covered the ground to break her husband's alibi. He was convicted but the Court of Criminal Appeal quashed the conviction saying they believed it to be unsafe. Springheeled Jack was a bogey figure of Victorian England, said to be able to leap walls in his attacks on women. One candidate for the title was the eccentric Marquis of Waterford. *Springheeled Jack* was also the title of a Victorian melodrama based on the story. 3. £5, Jack's alive = five. 4. heroin, Jack and Jill = pill. 5. alone, 'He's on his jack', Jack Jones = alone. 6. nothing = 'Can't do jack.' 7. to copulate. 8. (US) a blackjack. 9. Money. 10. (US pris) tobacco for hand-rolled cigarettes. 11. (mining) zinc. 12. to steal. 13. (Aus) the rectum. 14. venereal disease.

JACKET: (US) a case file of a criminal.

JACK IN THE BOX: 1. (US) housebreaking. 2. (Bl) the position during sexual intercourse when the penis is in the vagina.

JACK IT IN: 1. to stop. Often used as a command, 'Jack it in.' 2. to retire.

JACK MACK: (US pris) tinned fish, usually mackerel put in a sock and used as a weapon.

JACK OFF: 1. (UK) to masturbate. 2. (US) to pump the plunger of a hypodermic needle backwards and forwards resembling masturbation.

JACKPOT: (US) 1. serious trouble. 2. a maximum or severe sentence. 3. boastful recollections, 'Chopping up old jackpots again?' cf. cutting up touches.

JACK ROLLER: (US) a mugger of homosexuals, tramps and particularly drunks, poss. ex rolling lumberjacks. One of the most respected biographies of a criminal is *Memoirs of a Jack Roller*, often cited as a classic of research.

JACK THE BISCUIT: see Charlie Big Spuds.

JACK-UP: 1. to increase the price. 2. (Aus) to plead not guilty. 3. to refuse.

JACOB: a ladder, ex the Bible.

JAILBAIT: a sexually precocious girl under the age of consent. Twenty years ago the remark made to a man eyeing such a girl was, 'Fourteen gets you three.' Now community service would seem more likely.

JAKE: 1. methylated spirits. 2. (US) all right, 'Everything's Jake.' 3. trustworthy. 4. a police officer. 5. Jamaican ginger.

JAM: 1. (US BI) cocaine. 2. to sniff cocaine, 'We've been jamming all night,' ex music. 3. the vagina, ex menstruation, hence 4. sexual foreplay. 5. (UK) semen. 6. a heterosexual man, a term used by homosexuals. 7. trouble, a legal trap. 8. petty stolen goods, e.g. inexpensive watches, cigarette lighters etc.

JAM A PETE: (US) to fail to open the combination lock on a safe by failing to line up the tumblers correctly.

JAM BUTTY: (UK) a police car, ex the red stripe on white favoured by some police forces, or jam jar = car.

JAM FAG: a homosexual with no other real interest in life.

JAMMED: confronted.

JAMMED UP: (US) 1. arrested. 2. locked up for prison violations. 3. to be given additional time to serve by a Parole Board.

JAM RAGS: sanitary cloths.

JAM ROLL: parole.

JANE: a girl, 'Plain Jane'.

JARGOON: an Australian stone resembling a diamond which

could be used in a confidence trick or pennyweighting (qv).

J. ARTHUR; 1. masturbation, ex the film magnate, J. Arthur Rank = wank, because a character in *The Bofors Gun* says he is going for a J. Arthur and the film was banned on the Rank's Odeon circuit. The word is a good example of how the rhyming word is dropped. 2. a bank.

JAY; marijuana.

JAZZ; 1. the vagina. 2. sexual intercourse.

JEANS AT HALF MAST; (US) caught at a disadvantage, ex caught in the act of passive pederasty.

JEKYLL; fake goods, Jekyll and Hyde = snide.

JELLY; gelignite.

JELLYBEAN; (US) a pimp.

JELLY ROLL; 1. the vagina. 2. sexual intercourse. W.C. Handy, 'I'm most wile 'bout mah Jelly Roll', *St Louis Blues*. 3. a man

obsessed with sex, e.g. Ferdinand 'Jelly Roll' Morton.

JENNYBARN; (US) a low-quality brothel, often rooms attached to a bar.

JERK; (US) a foolish or inept person, ex a chronic masturbator.

JERK-OFF; to masturbate.

JERKWATER; (US pris) slow-witted.

JET; to run away.

JEWISH LIGHTNING; arson.

JEWISH PIANO; a cash register.

JEW'S TYPEWRITER; a cash register.

JIG OR JIGABOO; (US) an African-American.

JIGGER; (US) 1. a look-out often a man who watches in prison for informers whilst others carry out an illegal activity. 2. an exclamation of warning. 3. an armed robber. 4. a measure of spirits. 5. (Aus) A prison radio. 6.

any illegal device such as a battery attached to a whip for illegally stimulating a racehorse. 7. a truant.

JIGGLERS: skeleton keys.

JIG-JIG: sexual intercourse. Common in West African countries where bar girls, dressed in white, will spill into the car park seizing the testicles of potential clients asking, 'You jig-jig?'

JILL OFF: the politically correct term for female masturbation.

JIM: (US) to bungle.

JIMMER: 1. a man who spies on prostitutes or courting couples having sex outdoors. They operated particularly in parks and were tolerated by prostitutes as a form of protection against violent customers. 2. a person who obtains free entry to a greyhound meeting etc. or who occupies a better seat than the one he has paid for. When nude shows played at the Windmill Theatre in London, at the end of each performance men climbed over the seats in front of them to get nearer the stage. cf ligger.

JIMMIES: nerves, ex the English boxer who toured in Australia during World War One, Jimmy Britts = shits.

JIMMY: 1. a bar used for breaking and entering, a corruption of jemmy. 2. to force open. 3. (pris) foil used to 'run' heroin for smoking, ex the reformed criminal Jimmy Boyle = foil, 'Got any Jimmy?' 4. to urinate, ex Jimmy Riddle = piddle. 5. (Can) an injection of narcotics.

JIMSCREECH: to obtain entry into a flat or house by deceiving the owner, poss. ex jimmy.

JINNY: a bar room often linked to prostitution.

JIVE: (US Bl) 1. lies. 2. pretentiousness.

JIVE-ASS: a liar or false person.

JOB: 1. a criminal act. 2. to arrest. One police magazine was known as *The Job*.

JOCKER: 1. a young hobo in the power of an older, usually homosexual one 2. an active pederast.

JOCKEY; 1. a prostitute's client. The term is used in a derisory fashion by the women. 2. a contraceptive sheath.

JOCKNEY; a Scotsman who has spent too long in London.

JOE; (US) a gun.

JOE GHIRR; prison, ex Joe Ghirr = stir. Porridge, the staple prison breakfast, had to be stirred.

JOEY; 1. a parcel, usually drugs hidden on the person and brought into or out of prison, ex a kangaroo's young. 2. a young person bullied by an older one into stealing or mugging on his behalf. 3. (US) someone who takes the place at home of a person serving a prison sentence. 4. a silver 3d piece.

JOEYING; stealing from handbags.

JOHN; 1. a penis and therefore 2. a prostitute's client. 3. a contraceptive sheath. 4. an unknown person. John Doe was a legal fiction for bringing an action in certain civil courts, now 5. (US) an unidentified body. 6. an older homosexual protecting a younger one. 7. the lavatory, 'I'm going to see Cousin John.'

JOHN LAW; (UK) 1. a well-respected or senior police officer. 2. (US) the police in general.

JOHNNY; 1. a guard 2. a contraceptive sheath.

JOHNSON; 1. a prostitute's bully, ex the heavyweight boxing champion, Jack Johnson. 2. (US) a tramp or drifter.

JOHNSON BOYS; (US) a gang of thieves, ex a safebreaker's tool resembling a Johnson bar on an engine.

JOHNSON FAMILY, THE; (US) of, or well disposed towards, the Underworld, ex a legendary family of criminals including sheriffs who established protected or safe towns where criminals could live without fear of arrest provided they committed no crime in the town. Examples included Hot Springs, Arkansas and St Paul, Missouri.

JOHN THOMAS; the penis. D.H. Lawrence, *Lady Chatterley's Lover*.

JOINT; 1. prison. 2. the penis. 3. a marijuana cigarette. 4. any building but particularly a cheap restaurant or night club.

JOLLY BEANS; Benzedrine.

JOLT; (US) 1. to sentence to imprisonment. 2. death by electrocution.

JONES; a habit usually but not exclusively a drug habit.

JOTA; (Hisp pris) a homosexual, usually passive.

JOURNEY; penal servitude.

JOY RIDER; 1. a person who takes a motor car or is a passenger in one and then abandons it. 2. an occasional user of habit-forming drugs.

JOY TRAIL; the vagina. John Gregory Dunne, *True Confessions*, 'A votive candle up the joy trail.'

JUDY; a prostitute.

JUG; 1. prison, poss. ex the Scots *joug* = the pillory or Fr *joug* = yoke. 2. a bank.

JUGGED, TO BE; to be arrested and awaiting trial.

JUG HEAVY; (US) a specialist in blowing bank safe vaults.

JUGS; 1. breasts. 2. ears.

JUG UP; (Can) a prison meal.

JUICE; (US) 1. the current in the electric chair. 2. influence. 3. a bribe. 4. interest paid to a money-lender.

JUMP; 1. to mug or attack. 2. to have sexual intercourse, 'Are you going to jump my bones?' 3. to escape. 4. (Bl) to arrest.

JUMPED IN; (US) to be initiated into a gang.

JUMPED OUT; (US) to be allowed to leave a gang. This requires the survival of a beating by two or more members.

JUMPER; (UK) 1. a thief particularly one who steals from offices. 2. a ticket inspector on a train. 3. a wiring device used by burglars to divert an alarm system or to defeat a security device in a motor vehicle.

JUMPING CHINA; a partner in a prison escape attempt, ex china plate = mate.

JUMPING IN; (US) the initiation into a gang. It requires a beating to demonstrate bravery and fearlessness.

JUMP, THE; the counter area of banks, post offices and building societies.

JUMP UP; 1. to steal from the back of parked lorries by jumping up on the tailboard and handing down the contents. 2. to have sexual intercourse.

JUMP UP MERCHANT; 1. a specialist at the jump up. 2. a generally upwardly mobile young criminal.

JUNCTION, THE; the Clapham area of South London, ex the railway station.

JUNE BUG; (US) a prisoner who is regarded as a slave by others.

JUNGLE; 1. an area outside a town frequented by tramps. 2. a brothel district generally. The Jungle was an area of brothels and saloons behind the Brooklyn docks.

JUNK; (US) 1. narcotics. 2. any stolen goods excepting cash. 3. (UK) cheap or imitation jewellery.

JUNKER; (US) one addicted to narcotics.

JUNKIE; one addicted to narcotics.

JUNK TANK; (US) cells for alcoholics or drug addicts.

JUNKYARD DOG; an evil tempered or vicious person. 'He's mad as a junkyard dog.'

JURAS; (Sp pris) 1. police. 2. prison guard.

JURY'S OUT, THE; awaiting a decision, ex the retirement of a jury to consider the verdict.

K

K.: 1. a large amount of drugs, not necessarily a kilo. 2. Khat, a hallucinant narcotic chewed and common amongst East African communities.

KAMIKAZE MISSION: attempting a robbery without masks, often carried out by a junkie with a carrot in a bag.

KAMIKAZE MOVE: (US) a killing which takes place in front of a prison officer.

KANGAROO: (US) 1. a pimp. 2. prison tobacco, kangaroo = chew. 3. a prison warder, kangaroo = screw. 4. a Jewish person ex the same rhyming slang, often abb. to kanga.

KANGAROO COURT: (Can) prison disciplinary board. It does not appear to have any connection with Australia. At the beginning of 20c a kangaroo was either an unjust sentence or a mock trial held by inmates when the victim/defendant was accused of an offence such as child molestation.

KATHLEEN MAVOURNEEN: (Aus) an indeterminate sentence, ex the popular song, 'It may be for years, it may be never.'

K.C.: knowingly concerned, a catch-all in the drug laws which facilitates conviction, 'He's doing a twenty stretch for K.C.'

KEEP CAVVY; to keep a look-out. A corruption of the Latin *cave*. The usage is mostly schoolboy. *Cave canem*, beware of the dog, can still be found on house gates.

KEEP DIXIE; to keep a look-out, particularly for a three-card trick. Almost exclusively used on the Everton side of the Mersey. Dixie Dean was one of most popular members of the football club in the 1930s.

KEEP DOG; to keep a look-out. Again used particularly by three-card tricksters.

KEEP NIX; to keep a look-out. The use is largely confined to the Liverpool area.

KEEP SIX; (Can) to keep a look-out.

KEESTER; see Keister.

KEESTER BUNNY; (US) one who hides contraband in the rectum.

KEESTER SHAFTING; (US) anal intercourse.

KEISTER; (US) 1. a handbag. 2. a small safe. 3. the buttocks. 4. the rear trouser pocket, possibly ex (Eng) kist or chest or (Ger) *Kiste*, a place of concealment. The rectum has always been a place where valuables are concealed, see e.g. Henri Charrière, *Papillon*.

KEN; (Rom) a lodging house.

KETTLE; 1. a watch. A red kettle was a gold watch; a white kettle a silver one. Now used infrequently as a wristwatch. 2. To rob ex fairground slang. 3. (Can) a locomotive.

KETTLED; 1. drunk. 2. dead.

KEY; a kilo of drugs.

KHYBER; the buttocks, Khyber Pass = arse.

KIBITZER; a spectator at a card game, particularly one who offers unsought advice to a player.

KIBBLES AND BITS; crumbs of cocaine.

KICK; (US) 1. a pocket, particularly gambling slang, 'He put his bank-roll in his kick.' 2. a thrill, 'I get a kick out of you.' 3. (pl) shoes. 4. to get rid of, 'I kicked a hooker,' 'I got rid of a warrant.' 5. to break a drug habit. 6. to relax.

KICK ASS; to behave roughly to inferiors. Often used of police officers' conduct towards minority groups.

KICKBACK; (US) 1. a bribe or percentage of profit paid particularly to the police or government officials in return for favours received. 2. to make restitution, e.g. of stolen goods.

KICKER; (US) 1. a threat held over a prisoner, e.g. to prefer an extra charge if the man will not plead guilty. 2. a second concealed weapon in a robbery, and so 3. an advantage generally.

KICK OFF; (US) to die.

KICK OVER; (US) to refuse to submit to robbery or violence, ex kick over the traces, the refusal of a horse to be harnessed.

KICK THE HABIT; to break a narcotic addiction.

KICK, TO GO ON A; a prolonged period of drug taking.

KIDDY PORN; magazines and films featuring pictures of children in sexual positions.

KIFE; (US) 1. to swindle, ex carnival and circus. 2. to steal. (UK) 3. a bed. 4. a prostitute. 5. a passive or oral homosexual.

KIKE; a Jewish person, ex the practice at Ellis Island of immigrants to the United States. Those who could not write their names did not put a cross but drew a circle. When asked what it was the reply was a *kikel*.

KILL; to masturbate.

KILL A NUMBER; (US) to complete a prison sentence.

KILLING; (US) a prisoner who masturbates in public.

KILLING; 1. a large profit made in a short time often on the stock or commodity market. 2. (UK Bl) a mass robbery or fight.

KILLING BABIES; (US pris) masturbation.

KILO; a large amount of drugs, not necessarily that weight.

KIMONA; (US) a cheap usually pine coffin for burying prison inmates.

KINCHIN; a child or orphan beggar. In the late 19c children were kidnapped on a regular basis and forced to work as orphan beggars.

KING BUNG; (US) 1. a brothel keeper. 2. a White slaver.

KINKY; 1. stolen goods. 2. crooked or unfair. 3. to have unnatural sexual habits.

KINKY, TO BE K. OF; to be suspicious of, to dislike.

KIP; 1. a bed. 2. a lodging house or brothel. 3. to sleep. 4. (Aus) a bat used to throw the coins in a game of Two Up.

KIPPER; 1. (Aus and Can) an Englishman, ex two-faced, yellow-bellied and no guts. 2. a term of endearment.

KIPPY; (Aus) the tosser in a game of Two Up.

KISSER; the face.

KISS OF DEATH; the kiss given by a Mafia leader to an intended victim, ex the Bible.

KISS-OFF; to get rid of unwelcome company and specifically to get rid of the victim of a confidence trick.

KISS THE BABY; (US) a guaranteed sentence, 'He blew the peter now he's going to kiss the baby.'

KITE; 1. a cheque, originally a worthless bill of exchange. 2. (US) a letter with instructions smuggled by a prisoner to the outside.

KITING; passing stolen or worthless cheques.

KITTY; (US) prison.

KITTY KITTY; (US) a female prison officer.

KNEECAPPING; shooting or drilling a hole in the knee of a victim. A regular punishment imposed on informers by the IRA, kneecapping serves both as a punishment and a warning.

KNEE TREMBLE[R]; intercourse in the upright position, erroneously believed to be a form of contraception.

KNOB; 1. the penis. 2. the head. 3. (pl) breasts. 4. the Jack in a game of cribbage.

KNOBBER; a male homosexual transvestite. Chapman suggests it is either because of the false nipples or because the man gives knob jobs.

KNOB JOCKEY; (pris) a homosexual.

KNOCK; 1. to cheat or fail to pay a debt. 2. to disparage. 3. (UK) to have sexual intercourse. 4. to steal, common amongst Glasgow youth gangs.

KNOCKBACK: a refusal of parole or other form of early release.

KNOCKDOWN: a price below the true worth of the goods sold.

KNOCKER: (US) 1. the fist. 2. a drug addict who tries to break his habit. (UK) 3. someone who fails to pay a debt. 4. a person who makes disparaging remarks. 5. (pl) breasts. 6. testicles.

KNOCKINGS: the closing speeches in a criminal trial when one advocate gets to denigrate or knock the other's case.

KNOCKING SHOP: a brothel.

KNOCK OFF: 1. to steal. 2. to have sexual intercourse. 3. to kill. 4. to arrest.

KNOCK, ON THE: the practice of visiting houses to buy antiques, particularly from the elderly who can be cajoled or bullied into parting with their possessions at a knock-down price.

KNOCKOUT: to dispose cheaply of stolen goods or those acquired on credit, often quite openly in a shop used as a front (qv) for a long firm fraud (qv).

KNOCKOVER: to rob. Dashiell Hammett, *The Big Knockover*.

KNOCK UP: 1. to make pregnant. 2. to contaminate.

KNOW: (Aus) an individual giggle (qv), a small bribe.

KNOW NOTHINGS: derisory police term for a civilian.

KNUCKLE SANDWICH: a hard blow, particularly to the mouth.

KNUCKS: brass knuckles worn by enforcers.

KOKOMO: (US) a drug, particularly cocaine, addict.

KOSHER: genuine, reliable, ex Yiddish.

KOTCHEL: money, ex cotchel, a bundle. The modern use originated around Dewsbury, Yorkshire and has since acquired nationwide usage. Kotchel can be blue (£5), brown (£10), etc.

KOTCHELED, TO BE: (pris) to have plenty of something not necessarily money wanted by others.

KREMLIN: New Scotland Yard.

KURVA: a prostitute, ex Yiddish.

KWAY: (Aus) an all round, non-specialist thief.

L

LACE: 1. a prostitute, often lace mutton. 2. to beat, 'I gave him a good lacing.' 3. (SA) to be without money.

LADIES: (BI) prostitutes.

LADY: cocaine, reputedly a female aphrodisiac.

LAG: a prisoner, more often old lag or recidivist; originally a convict under sentence of transportation for seven years or more and an old lag who had been transported and returned home.

LAGGED. TO BE: to be sentenced.

LAGGER: (Aus) a police informer.

LAJARAS: (US) Hispanic name for the police, possibly a corruption of an officer named O'Hara.

LAMB DOWN: (Aus) to keep a victim drunk and so relieve him of his money, ex helping a ewe to give birth.

LAM. TO BE ON THE: (US) on the run from the police or prison, ex 16c Brit.

LAME. TO COME UP: to be unable to pay gambling debts.

LAMP: 1. to see or look 2. to hit in the face. 3. (pl) eyes or spectacles.

LAMPING: the practice of shining lights in the eyes of game whilst poaching at night.

LANDING: floors in a prison on which prisoners have their cells.

LARRIKIN: (Aus) a villain, often now almost a term of admiration. The popular 1920s criminal, Leslie 'Squizzy' Taylor, was described as Australia's Larrikin. An article in the *Sydney Morning Herald* (1974) described Dame Joan Sutherland as 'The heroine with a larrikin streak'.

LASH: (Aus) a trick or swindle.

LASHED UP: 1. burdened with somebody. 2. to be married, but more particularly to be in a temporary relationship.

LAST MILE; the walk to the gallows from the condemned cell. In recent years it has been an extremely short one. In Britain the gallows were placed next to the condemned cell and the executioner Albert Pierrepont would boast that he was able to take the man from the cell and hang him before the clock stopped striking nine.

LAUGH; (AUS) a large bribe to be shared between officers.

LAUGHING ACADEMY; (US) mental institution.

LAUNDER; to change dishonestly acquired money at a discount. In less sophisticated times this was done at the racetrack or across gaming tables and indeed it still is but now laundering has become an international and extremely sophisticated business involving the co-operation of banks, lawyers and accountants.

LAVENDER ALLEGATION; (US) an accusation of homosexuality, ex lavender water.

LAVENDER, TO BE IN THE; 1. dead. 2. (Russ) to be arrested.

LAVENDER, TO LAY IN; 1. to hide. 2. (US) to kill.

LAWING; see corner.

LAY; 1. to have sexual intercourse. 2. a woman considered only in sexual terms, 'She's a good lay.'

LAY DOWN; a remand in custody, often for mental, medical and social inquiry reports.

LAY HIM DOWN; to kill.

LAY ON THE HIP; to smoke opium, ex the comfortable position assumed.

LAY PAPER; to pass worthless cheques.

LAY TRACK; (US) to lie, specifically to other prison inmates.

LEAD POISONING; (US) gunshot wounds.

LEADAKE; see skimming.

lay off

LEATHER: 1. a wallet. 2. the anus.

LEBANESE LOOP: a method of stealing cards from cash machines.

LEE MARVIN: hungry, Lee Marvin = starving.

LEGGNER: a sentence of one year.

LEG HANGER: (US) a prisoner who associates with the guards.

LEG IT: to run away from the police.

LEGIT: honest, straight.

LEG OVER, TO HAVE A: 1. to swindle. 2. to have sexual intercourse.

LEGSHAKE ARTIST: (Aus) a pickpocket.

LEG UP DEFENCE: a defence which needs the co-operation of the defending solicitor in its construction, 'Do you need a leg up brief?' = 'Do you need a dishonest solicitor?'

LEMAC: (US) a Camel cigarette, backslang.

LEMON: 1. cocaine, ex lemon barley = charlie. 2. a fool. A Borstal insult, 'That man's a proper lemon,' poss. ex a former Borstal boy, Fred Lemon, who claimed he saw Jesus in the punishment block at Portland. He is said later to have become a vicar and written a book about his experiences.

LENO: (Sp pris) a marijuana joint.

LETTUCE: (US) 1. paper money. 2. prisoners who will embark on gang rape.

LEVEL, ON THE: 1. straight, honest. 2. flat as opposed to jump racing.

LF: see Long Firm Fraud.

LIBERTY: an unfair advantage taken of someone, often the speaker. The next degree is a right liberty and the most outrageous behaviour is diabolical liberty, a situation which occurs when the other person is out of order (qv).

LICK; a blow, 'I gave him a good lick.'

LIFE, THE; pimping and prostitution generally.

LIFER; 1. a prisoner serving a sentence of life imprisonment. 2. a prison officer, used by themselves.

LIGGER; a person who, uninvited, attends premieres, parties, launches etc.

LINE, ON THE; (Aus) under police observation.

LINEN; a newspaper, linen draper = paper.

LINER; (UK BI) a policeman, particularly a member of a pickpocket squad.

LINE-UP; (US) an identification parade.

LIQUIDATE; to kill.

LIQUID ECSTASY; the date-rape drug GHB (gamma hydroxybutrate).

LITTLE BARBARY; Wapping, London, ex the danger.

LITTLE JOE; (US) a method of killing reserved for loan shark debtors and welshers (qv). The victim is shot four times in the head in two rows.

LITTLE JOE IN THE SNOW; (US) cocaine, ex snow = blow.

LITTLE MAN; 1. clitoris. 2. a cigarette.

LITTLE MAN IN A BOAT; the clitoris, ex the supposed resemblance.

LITTLE POSITION, A; in trouble with the police. *The Times Magazine* 17 November 2001.

LIVE HOOK UP; a call made from prison.

LIVERPOOL KISS; a blow to the mouth.

LIVERPOOL LEG; urination in another's trouser pocket. It is said to have originated at football matches when, because of a lack of lavatory facilities coupled with a desire not to miss the game, it became a practice to relieve oneself in a neighbour's coat or trouser pocket.

LIVIN'; (UK Bl) a person.

LIVIN' DRUM, TO DO A; (UK Bl) to commit a household burglary.

LOADED; to be full of 1. money. 2. drink. 3. drugs.

LOAN SHARK; an unlicensed moneylender who lends at extortionate rates, very often the seemingly innocuous six for five. For £5 borrowed one week £6 must be repaid the next. The interest rate is staggering.

LOCKDOWN; the highly unpopular practice of confining prisoners to their cell, done at the time of emergency to avoid trouble. In American prisons a lockdown can continue for several weeks.

LOID; celluloid, ex the silent film star Harold Lloyd.

LOLLY; 1. to inform, ex lollypop = shop. 2. money.

LONG FIRM FRAUD; the setting up of a business designed to obtain money on credit and then to disappear with the proceeds of sale.

LONG GREEN; paper money.

LONG ONE; £100, sometimes £1,000.

LONG ROD; a rifle.

LOOGAN; 1. (US) a gunman. 2. (Can) a mentally ill prisoner.

LOON; (Aus) a pimp.

LOOP JOINT; an arcade which shows a continuous chain of sex films. The punter must feed in a succession of coins for say two minutes' worth of film and the aim of the manager is to ensure that the time runs out at a crucial part of the action so forcing the viewer to insert more coins. In effect they are an expensive and adult version of What the Butler Saw, beloved of pier visitors between the wars.

LOOT; money or goods, usually illegally obtained, ex Urdu.

LOW HEEL; (Aus) a woman of

dubious reputation, a prostitute. The heels of her shoes are worn down from walking the pavements.

LUCK OUT; (US) 1. to be extremely lucky. 2. to be extremely unlucky, finished.

LUMBER; 1. to arrest or imprison. 2. to take advantage of another's kindness, and so 3. (Scots) a girl taken to her home after a dance. 4. (US) spectators in a casino.

LUMP; cannabis.

LUMP, THE; a building site fraud to avoid payment of income tax.

LUNCH-BASKET (BOX); the penis and testicles together.

LUNCH, TO BE OUT TO; (US) 1. extremely stupid, mental. 2. in the wrong, behaving badly.

LUSH; a drunk, ex Lushington, a 19c brewery.

LUSH ROLLER; (US) a pick-pocket who specialises in stealing from drunks.

LUTHER; a prison visit, ex the footballer Luther Blissett = visit.

LYNCHING; an extra judicial hanging, prob. either ex Colonel William Lynch who set out to clear Pittsburgh County, Va. of an unruly element or Charles Lynch who, with his brother, founded Lynchburg, Va. The first lynching seems to have taken place in 1780.

*145
the lowdown*

M: 1. morphine. 2. marijuana.

MAC(K): a pimp, ex Fr maque-reau.

MACE: 1. to get something for nothing. 2. to throw spice in the eyes of a victim during a robbery. 3. to cheat or steal.

MACK: (US gang) a weapon.

MADAM: 1. to tell lies, ex Madame de Luce = spruce (qv). 2. to tell a tale or flatter, 'Don't madam me.'

MADE MAN: a person inducted into a Mafia family.

MAG: (US) a prison officer.

MAGAZINE: 1. (UK) a six-month prison sentence, ex the time it took a person with little education to read a book. 2. (US) sixty days. There is clearly less illiteracy in America.

MAGGIE: a matron at a Borstal institution.

MAGGIE MAGGIE: (Aus) an automatic pistol.

MAGGOT: (US Bl) a White person.

MAGSMAN: originally a high-class well-dressed swindler but now a petty thief.

MAINLINE: to inject drugs into a vein.

MAIN SQUEEZE: (US) 1. a particular girlfriend. 2. (Bl) a main drug connection.

MAKE: 1. to induct into the Mafia. 2. to recognise or identify. 3. to have sexual intercourse. 4. to steal or rob.

MAKE ONE: to escape from prison.

MAKE PAPER: (US) 1. to counterfeit. 2. to be given parole.

MALLEE ROOT: (Aus) a prostitute. Mallee was an Aboriginal word for a species of eucalypt. A mallee was also a Black person who had adopted the Christian religion.

MAMA BEAR: (US) a policewoman.

MAMMY: (US) an abundance, so a person with an amount of tobacco has tobacco mammy.

MANOR: a district or territory marked out by the police or criminals as opposed to a postal district, 'I'm not having thieving on my manor.' 'He was off his manor.'

MAN TRAP: the vagina.

MAP: 1. the face. 2. (US) a cheque, 'Don't take his map, he's a paper hanger (qv).

MAQUEREAU: (Fr) a low-life figure, specifically a pimp.

MAQUERELLE: (Fr) a procuress.

MARATHON: (US) a long evening for a call girl. It will involve dinner and dancing before intercourse with the client.

MARBLE ORCHARD: (US) a prison graveyard.

MARICON: (Sp pris) 1. a homosexual. 2. an inmate with no courage.

MARK: 1. (US) the victim of a confidence trick. 2. (Aus) a boy, ex Mark Foy = boy.

MARKER: 1. a signed promissory note. 2. a favour which requires one in return, 'He's calling in his markers.'

MARK POINTS: to keep watch in order to assess the potential of a time and place for theft or robbery.

MARMACHA: (Sp pris) an active dominant lesbian.

MARRIED, TO BE: to have joined a street gang.

MATILDA, TO HAVE A: to defecate.

MATTRESS, TO GO TO THE: (US) to be at war with a rival gang, ex putting down mattresses on the floor in temporary lodgings.

MAU MAU: (US) a Black prison gang, ex the Kenyan gang of the 1950s.

MAX OUT; (US) to serve an entire sentence.

MAYTAG; (US) 1. a weak prisoner unable to protect himself from homosexual rape, and so 2. to commit an act of homosexual rape. 3. a passive homosexual partner. (Texas usage).

MCMUFF; (US) the vagina, ex the fast-food chain.

MEAT; the penis.

MEAT, TO BEAT (FLOG); masturbation.

MEAT EATER; 1. a police officer who will actively seek bribes. 2. a prostitute who will perform fellatio.

MEAT RACK; a place of homosexual prostitution, e.g. London's Piccadilly Circus.

MEAT SALESMAN; (US) a pimp.

MEAT WAGON; (US) a police van used to round-up prostitutes and take them to the station.

MEC; (Fr) a pimp or general low-life character, (abb. *maquereau).*

MECCA; Harlem, New York.

MECHANIC; 1. a hired killer. 2. an expert, but usually dishonest, card player who uses sleight of hand.

MECHANICAL STOOL PIGEON; (US) a walk-through metal detector.

MECHANIC'S GRIP; a method of holding a deck of cards with three fingers curled along the length of the card and the index finger at the narrow upper edge away from the body.

MEET; a meeting arranged by a criminal's confidant, often with a police officer or another intermediary, to discuss terms of bail; now more usually what evidence will be given at trial and what, for a fee, may be suppressed. It can also refer to a meeting by a policeman with an informant. Again money will inevitably change hands at some stage.

MEETS, THE; a conference of leading Underworld figures.

MEMPHIS DOMINOES; dice.

MERCY ROOM; (US) the emergency room at a hospital.

MERKIN; a pubic wig worn originally when the victim was suffering from lice. Apparently it was fairly common in South Africa as late as the 1950s. In Stanley Kubrick's *Dr Strangelove* the United States' President was named Merkin Muffley.

MET, THE; the Metropolitan Police.

METH CHARGE; (US) child molestation. 'I was only mething around.'

METHODIST; a two-headed axe used in a lumbercamp, ex the supposed unreliability of John Wesley's followers.

MEXICAN BROWN; a superior type of marijuana.

MIDDLE; (US) 1. a guaranteed winning bet. 2. (UK) to involve another to his detriment, James Morton, *Gangland: The Lawyers*, 'I've never middled a solicitor in my life.'

MIDDLING; (US) selling stolen goods.

MILASA; (Sp pris) a prison officer, ex *milasa* = syrup. Prison officers are regarded as slow-witted.

MING; the police, ex Ming the Merciless, the evil opponent of Flash Gordon.

MING ON THE WING; the police are coming.

MINK; (US Bl) a feral sexy woman, or less usually a man. Less common than foxy.

MISS EMMA; morphine.

MISSION; (US) 1. a contract hit; 2. a drive-by shooting.

MITT; (US) 1. a hand, and therefore 2. a hand of cards. 3. to arrest. 4. (pl) handcuffs.

MITT JOINT; a fortune teller's booth.

M.O.; *modus operandi*, the particular way in which a criminal regularly commits his crimes.

MOCKERDY: (Romany) something impure.

MOCKERS, TO PUT THE M. ON: to bring bad luck, ex Yiddish.

MODPLOD: a Ministry of Defence police officer.

MOGGIES: amphetamines.

MOLL: 1. (Aus) a prostitute 2. a girlfriend or sweetheart but one who often associates with criminals.

MOLLY, (MISS): an effete homosexual.

MONEY: (US pris) 1. a trusted or best friend. 2. goods which can be traded since money is not permitted.

MONKEY: 1. £500. 2. a large padlock.

MONKEY'S, NOT TO GIVE A: not to care, poss. ex powder monkey boy used to load cannons in naval warfare and therefore highly expendable.

MONSTER; HIV, 'He's got the Monster.'

MONSTER MANSION, THE; HMP Wakefield, ex the high number of sex offenders held there.

MONTE: (NZ) a certainty.

MOONLIGHTING: the police practice of taking a second job without permission. In one well-known case a constable faced dismissal when it was found his wife was running a seaside bed and breakfast. He avoided proceedings when he was able to show that the assistant chief constable who was chairing the disciplinary board was running a computer consultancy a mile from police headquarters.

MOOR, THE: HMP Dartmoor.

MOTHERFUCKER: once a serious term of abuse but now an all-purpose word.

MOUSE: 1. a bruise under the eye. 2. (US) a police informer.

MOUTHPIECE: a lawyer, very often a dishonest one.

MOVE: a scheme or scam.

MR WHIPPLE: (US Bl) PCP

moneymaker

mixed with embalming fluid.

MR WOOD: a police truncheon carried in a special deep pocket, 'May I introduce you to my friend Mr Wood?'

MSB: (US gang) money, sex, bitches.

MUFF: the female pubic hair.

MUFF-DIVING: cunnilingus.

MUG(G): 1. a crude, rough thief, orig. 19c. 2. a policeman. 3. a homosexual, poss. ex the meaning dupe, the victim of the blackmailer. 4. a convict. 5. to rob, usually in the street, of jewellery or valuables.

MUGGLE: (US) Marijuana.

MUG SHOT: a police photograph. In the late 19c, pushing the mugs around was slang for showing photographs of suspected criminals.

MULE: a drug courier.

MULLIGAN: stew served in prison.

MULLIGANS: (Aus) doctored playing cards.

MUMP HOLE: a place where police can eat without payment etc.

MUMPING: the police practice of obtaining discounts or free meals from local traders in return for implicit protection of their premises. Mumping is regarded either as a perk of the job or very low on the scale of corruption, ex 17c to mump = to beg.

MUPPET: 1. a lay, or unqualified, magistrate. 2. a uniformed policeman (plain clothes use).

MURPHY GAME: 1. the beating and robbing of a prostitute's client. 2. a confidence trick in which a punter is sent around a corner to await delivery of goods or a girl, which or who will never arrive, ex the alleged simplicity of the Irish.

MUSH: 1. the mouth. 2. a prostitute's client (mainly Liverpool). 3. a friend or mate, in which case the word is pronounced with a short 'u'.

MUSHROOM; (US gang) an innocent bystander victim in a drive-by shooting.

MUSTACHE PETE; an old-fashioned Sicilian member of the Mafia in the early 20c and regarded as largely out of touch. Lucky Luciano is said to have eliminated the Mustachio Petes across America in a night of the Sicilian Vespers in September 1931.

MUTI; (SA) the practice of selling children for their body parts.

MUTT; deaf, ex Mutt and Jeff.

MYSTERY; 1. a girl, specifically a virgin, 'It's a mystery how she's still a virgin.' It is possible that it derives from a popular radio programme in which contestants had to guess 'a mystery word' = bird. 2. a mystery may also be a stray girl, possibly a runaway living rough in London. The mystery was how she survived. 3. (US) a crime, difficult if not impossible to solve.

N

NAB; 1. to arrest. 2. (BI) a policeman.

NAIL; 1. to rob or steal. 2. to seize, 'The pigs frisked my panney and nailed my screws' = 'The police searched my house and seized my picklock keys.' 3. to arrest, ex nail down. 4. to obtain sufficient evidence to secure a conviction. 5. a cigarette, abb. coffin nail.

NAK; nose, ex Romany.

NAMBLING; gambling on the Internet. Jerry Raines, *Small Change*.

NANCY; the buttocks.

NANCY BOY; an effete homosexual, one who favours the buttocks.

NARK; an informer, ex nak (qv).

NASH; 1. to run away. 2. a call that a crime is being interrupted.

NAUTCH; the vagina, ex Hindi.

NAZI LOW RIDER; an American White right-wing prison gang.

NEAR BEER JOINT; a club where patrons are led to believe they are drinking champagne and that sex is available. They are wrong.

NEBBISH; (Yiddish) a complete loser.

NECKINGS; (Aus) robbery by strangulation.

NECKTIE; the hangman's noose.

NEEDLE; 1. a hypodermic syringe. 2. ill feeling.

NEEDLE MATCH; a boxing or other contest where there is real or feigned bad feeling between the contestants. The punters now believe they are getting something extra for their money.

NEDDY; a cosh.

NERDY; tedious and contemptible.

NESTER; a member of the prison gang Nuestra Familia (Our Family).

NETA; a powerful Hispanic prison gang, originally formed in Puerto Rico but now strong on the East Coast of America.

NETTIE; an outside lavatory, poss. ex a contraction of the necessary.

NEVADA GAS; (US) cyanide.

NEVES; (backslang) seven.

NEWINGTON BUTTS; the stomach, butts = guts.

N.F.A.; no fixed abode. A reason for refusing bail.

NICK; 1. to steal, poss. ex 18c from a nick-pot, a beer mug with a false bottom so the customer received less than he paid for; poss. ex Old Nick, the Devil. 2. to arrest. 3. a police station.

NICK, IN GOOD; in good shape or condition.

NICKEL; five years, ex five cents.

NIFTY; 1. £50. 2. insolent, cocky. 3. odorous.

NIFTY, A BIT OF; sexual intercourse.

NIGGER MINSTREL; durophet capsule.

NIGHTHAWK; burglar.

NIGHT TROTS; (NZ) floodlit trotting races.

NIPPERS; 1. handcuffs. 2. small children.

NINJA; HIV.

NITTO; an expression of annoyance or surprise, 'Nitto. I've only gone and got a ten.'

NIX; nothing, ex German *Nichts*.

NOB; 1. the penis. 2. a member of the upper strata of society. 3. the knave in a suit of cards in Cribbage.

NOBBLE; 1. to interfere with, particularly a member of a jury by threats or bribery. 2. to injure or dope a horse or greyhound.

NOD; the verdict.

NOD, ON THE; 1. the drowsy state following an injection of narcotics. 2. a very close finish to a horse race when the horse which literally nods its head on the line gets the verdict. 3. not monitored, 'on the quiet'.

NODDING AND SMILING; male solicitation in a public lavatory, 'I watched the defendant, his erect penis in his hand, nod and smile at the man in the next stall.'

NODDY; a uniformed policeman, ex the Enid Blyton character.

NODDY BIKE; a velocette motorcycle capable of a top speed of forty mph used by the police and designed to allow officers to cover three or four beats and so compensate for a lack of manpower, again ex the Enid Blyton character.

NOD THE NUT; (Aus) to admit or plead guilty.

NO FT; reply by a suspect interviewed by a police officer meaning no comment, ex the long-running advertisement by the Financial Times, 'No FT. No comment'.

NOISE; heroin.

NONCE; a child molester, poss. ex a little bit of nonsense, a prison euphemism for the crime committed.

NONCING; 1. child molestation. 2. passing stolen cheques. A term used in the Home Counties in the 1960s but never more widely used.

NO NECK; a fool.

NOOKIE; sexual intercourse.

NOSE; 1. a detective. 2. a police informer, ex Romany *nak* = nose.

NOSE BAG, TO HAVE ONE'S N. ON; to eat, ex horse racing.

NOSE CANDY; cocaine, sometimes heroin because it is sniffed.

NOSH; 1. food. 2. to steal selectively.

NOSH ROD; a fork.

NOTICE: a contract to hurt or kill.

NUGGET: the new prison word for hobbit (qv).

NUMBER, TO HAVE SOMEONE'S: to know a secret from a person's past and thereby be able to exert financial or other pressure.

NUMBERS RACKET: illegal American lottery begun in the 19c principally by White operators which died with the arrest and conviction of the numbers king, Adams. From then until the 1920s it was principally a Harlem-based racket before the mobster Arthur Fleigenheimer, known as Dutch Schultz, seized it by force. Based on daily horse racing or stock exchange results and run on the lines of a football pool, a winning number is paid at 600-1 when the true odds are 900-1. Over twenty million people are said to play the numbers racket annually with a turnover of billions. The numbers game is relatively easy to fix so that big payouts are avoided.

NUT: 1. the expenses incurred by thieves setting up a theft or robbery, e.g. payment for a stolen car etc. 2. a bribe given to a police officer or other public figure. 3. the principal sum advanced by a loan shark as opposed to the vigorish (qv) . 4. the head. 5. to head butt. 6. (pl) the testicles.

NUT AND GUT REPORTS: mental and medical reports required by a court to determine a defendant's fitness to stand trial or be sentenced to prison.

NUT HOUSE: mental hospital.

NUTTER: a mentally unstable person; one who acts unpredictably. 'He's a right nutter.'

O

187; (US gang) as graffiti a death threat, ex the police code for murder.

O; opium.

OBBO; police observation on criminals.

OBLIGE; to kill, Frank Fraser, *Mad Frank's Diary*, 'In this last month alone I've even had two offers for me to oblige someone.'

OCHRE; money, ex the colour of gold.

O.D.; drug overdose.

ODD; the police, particularly detectives.

ODDLOT; a police car, particularly in use in the 1960s.

ODDS IT; to be unable to avoid.

OFAY; Black term of abuse for a White person, poss. ex corruption of foe.

OFFICE, THE; 1. a warning, tip off. 2. an instruction, 'The horse quickened as soon as he was given the office.'

OFF THE CUFF; impromptu.

OLD ARMY GAME; a swindle or trick.

OLD BILL; the police.

OLD LADY; 1. wife. 2. mother.

OLD MAN; 1. a husband. 2. a father. 3. a term of endearment for old friend.

OLD SMOKEY; the electric chair, ex the smoke issuing from the head and body of the victim during a botched exececution.

OL' SPARKEY; the electric chair in Florida. When the mass murderer Ted Bundy was executed in 1989 part of the waiting crowd sang, 'On top of ol' Sparkey'.

ON A PROMISE; 1. awaiting money in the form of a bribe or reward for information or services performed. It may apply either to the police or criminals. The promise is often not forthcoming. 2. to go on a date. The implication is that sex will be available at the end of the evening.

ONCER: £1.

ON DAB: to be on a police disciplinary charge.

ONE TRICK PONY: a person with a single talent.

ON MY SKIN: (US pris) on my word, on my life.

ONNER: £100.

ON ONE: to behave outrageously due to drink or drugs.

ON THE ARM: to obtain goods or food without paying, particularly applicable to the police. If done by criminals it is called extortion.

ON THE FLY: in a hurry.

ON THE GAME: prostitution.

ON THE JOB: 1. the act of committing a crime. 2. the act of sexual intercourse.

ON THE KNOCK: the practice of knocking on doors with the intention of persuading homeowners, particularly the elderly and vulnerable, to sell antiques for less than their true value.

ON THE LAM: (US) on the run from prison or the police.

ON THE NUMBERS, TO BE: the protection wing of a prison where child molesters are held.

ON THE ONE: honest, ex George Washington, who could not tell a lie, on a $1 bill.

ON THE PAD: wholesale bribery in a scheme in which criminals will pay a set fee to a police station weekly or monthly to be shared between officers according to rank and length of service.

ON TOP: the cry of a look-out, someone is coming.

ON YOUR TOD: to be alone, ex the American 19c jockey Tod Sloan = alone. He finished so far in front of other jockeys.

OPP(O): 1. opposition. 2. a partner, ex the opposite number on a ship.

ORCHESTRAS: testicles, ex orchestra stalls = balls.

ORPHAN PAPER: (US) bad cheques.

OSCAR: 1. a pistol. 2. (Aus) cash, ex Oscar Ashe, the original star of the musical *Chu Chin Chow*.

OUT, AN: a potentially winning defence to a criminal charge often arranged by the police in return for information or money.

OUT IN THE WATER: (US) in debt.

OUT OF ORDER: in the wrong, behaving badly, taking an unfair advantage. 'He was totally out of order so I gave him a smack (qv).'

OUTSIDE, THE: prison term for the outside world.

OUTSIDE MAN: watchman outside a building to give the alarm of any coming police; a look-out man for a three-card trick team.

OUT TO LUNCH: totally in the wrong; crazy.

OVERS: proceeds of crime not yet divided up.

OVER THE BLUE WALL: (US) confined to a hospital for the criminally insane.

OVER THE WALL, TO GO: to escape from prison.

OX: (US pris) a razorblade.

OXFORD: five shillings in the days when there were four dollars to the pound, ex Oxford scholar.

OYABUN: the Godfather of a Japanese gang.

OYSTER: a society woman employed to wear stolen jewellery in the hope she will receive an offer from a fence. Because of her social position she will not be suspected by the police.

P

PACHUCOS; a long-standing Hispanic street gang formed in the 1940s and involved in the Zoot Suit riots in Los Angeles.

PACK; 1. heroin. 2. to carry a weapon, esp. a gun, 'He's packing heat.' 3. to conceal in the rectum.

PACKAGE, TO HAVE THE TOTAL; to have AIDs.

PACKET; 1. a substantial sum of money, 'The brief cost me a packet.' 2. a wound.

PACK RAT; a small-time thief.

PAD; 1. a flat or room. 2. a list of names to whom bribes are paid. 3. a cell used for violent inmates.

PADDING; the police practice of adding to the quantity of drugs actually seized to upgrade an arrest.

PAD OF STITCHES; (US BI) hospital.

PALM OIL; a bribe.

PAN; 1. to beg, ex panhandle when beggars held out tin cups or plates. 2. to denigrate. 3. to strike.

PANDILLAS; (Sp pris) a prisoner who will plunder another's cell.

PANGY; £5, ex Romany.

PAN OUT; (US) to end, 'I don't know how it will pan out,' ex mining when pans were shaken to see if there were gold nuggets amongst the shale and stones scooped from the river.

PAPER HANGER; (US) passer of forged cheques or banknotes.

PARALYTIC; hopelessly drunk.

PAROLE DUST; fog, ex the better opportunity for an escape.

PASTE; (US) semen.

PASTEL; (US) an unmarked police car.

PAT; (Aus) a Chinaman.

PATCH; 1. prison or motorcycling gang insignia. 2. (US) an amount of money to be given to a corrupt police officer for protection.

PATCHES; fluorescent yellow patches sewn on the prison uniform of potential escapers.

PAVEMENT ARTIST; a robber specialising in wages snatches from vans delivering money to banks.

PAVEMENT PRINCESS; a prostitute.

PAY OFF; 1. profit-sharing by criminals. 2. a regular bribe paid to police or prison warders.

PAYOLA; bribery. One form was the payment by record companies to disc jockeys to play their records on radio shows.

PC HARD; the officer who will interrogate a suspect roughly threatening him with violence to obtain a confession. If this treatment is not successful his partner, PC Soft, will take over offering sympathy and cigarettes.

PEACE OUT; (US gang) goodbye, see you later.

PEACH; 1. to inform 2. the anus.

PECKER; the penis.

PECKER PALACE; a place in prison for conjugal visits. Unknown in Britain.

PECKERWOOD; (US) derogatory prison term for a White inmate.

PEDIGREE; criminal record.

PEELER; a police officer, ex Sir Robert Peel founder of the Metropolitan Police in 1829. Now used almost exclusively in Northern Ireland. 2. a prison officer, North Country use.

PEEPER; 1. an eye. 2. a detective, usually a private detective specialising in divorce work.

PEN; prison, abb. the penitentiary.

PENCIL; the penis.

PENMAN; a forger. The barrister James Sayward, one of the most talented, and the first in a long line of forgers, known as Jim the Penman, helped dispose of the gold from the First Great Train Robbery in 1854.

PENNYWEIGHTING; stealing by palming a piece of jewellery and then fixing it under the customer's side of the counter to be collected later by an accomplice.

PEOPLE; (US pris) family or close friends.

PEPPER AND SALT ACT; a lesbian display between a Black and a White girl.

PERCHER; 1. a shoplifter. 2. an easy arrest or victim.

PERICO(A); (US) heroin.

PERP; (US) suspect, abb. perpetrator.

PETER; 1. a safe. 2. a prison cell. (US) 3. a chest or portmanteau. 4. the penis.

PETERMAN; safebreaker.

PETER PUFFER; (US) homosexual who practises oral sex.

PHONE; a prison lavatory. If emptied it can be used as an in-house telephone.

PICCOLO PLAYER; homosexual or prostitute who practises oral sex.

PICK UP; to steal from unattended cars.

PIECE; (US) 1. a gun. 2. a woman.

PIECE OF THE BUSINESS; a share of profits from a crime family's business.

PIECE OF WORK; a term of admiration.

PIE EATER; (Aus) small-time criminal.

PIG; a police officer, UK 19c originally used wholly for detectives but now a general term of abuse worldwide.

PIG BROTHER; (US Bl) an informer, especially to White authorities.

PIGEON; a criminal's target, ex something to be plucked.

PIGEON DROP: one of the standard and most lasting confidence tricks in which the victim believes he will be able to share in the proceeds of an apparently stuffed wallet found in the street. The trick with variations is most common in the United States and requires an element of greed by the victim.

PIKER: a small-time cheat.

PIKEY: a gypsy, ex one who frequented turnpikes.

PILL: 1. a cigarette. 2. an annoying person. 3. (US) a bullet.

PILLOW BITER: passive homosexual, ex the position and pain of anal entry.

PIMP: 1. a man who lives off the immoral earnings of prostitutes. 2. (Aus) a police informer.

PIMP DUST: cocaine.

PIN: a female keeping look-out on behalf of other prisoners. 'She's a pin.' 'Keep pin for us.'

PINCH: to arrest.

PINGED, TO BE: (Aus biker) being spotted by a laser or speed camera.

PINKIE: 1. (Aus) cheap wine, 2. (US) a White person.

PINKTOES: (US) a White person but often used as a term of endearment.

PINEAPPLE: a bomb.

PIPE: 1. to see, listen to or notice. 2. to cry, abb. pipe the eye.

PIPES: the vocal cords, 'Frank Sinatra had great pipes.'

PIRATING: operating a lorry without an 'A' licence.

PISS AND WIND, TO BE FULL OF: to brag.

PISS IN A POCKET: (Aus) to cajole or flatter.

PISS IT OUT THE WINDOW: to waste money, often said by criminals who have squandered proceeds on cars and women instead of investing.

PIT: a bed.

PITCH; 1. a site used by street vendors, three-card tricksters and prostitutes. 2. sales talk, and therefore 3. (US) the proposition-ing of a woman, 'Any minute now he'll make a pitch.'

PITCHER; (US) the active part-ner in a homosexual act.

PITS; ugly, disgusting.

PLANT; 1. a cache of narcotics. 2. to put stolen goods or drugs in a suspect's pocket or in his possession and thereby provide false evidence against him. 3. (US) a person on the scene of a crime but remaining hidden.

PLASTERED; drunk, poss. ex Plaster of Paris = Aris = Aristotle = bottle.

PLASTIC, ON THE; using stolen credit cards to defraud banks and businesses.

PLATER; 1. a woman or homo-sexual man who will practise oral intercourse. 2. a person of little worth, ex a poor quality race-horse that will only run in selling plates where the winner is auctioned after the race.

PLAY A MATINEE; to cheat or steal from the same victim twice in a day.

PLAYER; a member of a team of confidence tricksters.

PLAYHOUSE; (Bl) the vagina, 'Her playhouse done burned down' = 'She has contracted VD.'

PLAYING ON ASS; (US) to gamble without money to pay any losses.

PLAY THE MOUTH ORGAN; to use a match-box cover to take drugs.

PLAY THE PIANO; to have one's fingerprints taken, ex the pressing and position of each finger.

PLEBE, LA; (Sp) the gang.

PLOD (MR); a uniformed police-man, ex the Enid Blyton charac-ter, the police generally.

PLOT UP; to park a police observation car.

PLUG; 1. (US) to shoot. 2. very, 'She's plug ugly.'

PLUM: an unintelligent person, ex Little Plum in the *Beano* comic, a Borstal insult.

PLUMA: (Sp) prostitute.

POCKET MAN: (US) a criminal trusted to hold the proceeds of crime before a shareout.

POKE: 1. a wallet. 2. to have sexual intercourse. 3. to punch.

POKEY: prison.

POKIES: (Aus) poker machines, the staple income of Australian clubs.

POLEFISHING: see Angler.

POLE PLEASER: (US pris) a passive homosexual.

POLIS: (Scots) the police.

POLLO: an illegal Mexican immigrant to the United States, ex Spanish chicken because the immigrants are plucked by bandits operating on the US–Mexican border.

PONCE: a man who lives off the immoral earnings of women, originally a younger man kept by a woman.

PONTOON: 21 months' imprisonment, occasionally 21 years.

PONY: 1. £ 25, poss. ex the price once paid for a small horse. 2. defecation, ex pony and trap = crap. (US) 3. a chorus or showgirl, ex the prancing movement of a chorus line. 4. trash or inferior goods.

PONY AND TRAP: once criminal slang for silver goods from the theory that as silver is to gold so is a pony and trap to a motor car.

PONY UP: to pay.

POOFTER: an effete person probably homosexual, poss. ex World War One a person who smoked cigarettes and not the more manly pipe.

POOGIE: (US) prison.

POON(TANG): the vagina now a woman generally. Originally Southern American and referring to a person of colour now more general use, ex Fr putain.

POOP BUTT; (US Bl) a person not to be trusted.

POP A WINDOW; a smash and grab raid.

POPPY LOVE; an elderly Jewish male.

PORK; 1. a corpse, ex the resemblance to the colour of a side of pork. 2. the penis. 3. to have sexual intercourse.

PORK PACKER; a necrophiliac, attributed to undertakers. Necrophilia is not a crime in England and Wales.

PORRIDGE; prison, ex the staple diet. It was said that if a prisoner did not eat his porridge on the last morning of his sentence he would return to prison.

PORTSMOUTH DEFENCE; the justification of the robbing of a homosexual by a sailor. The rationale was that the man was so appalled by the approach that he felt obliged to kick and beat him. Why he also felt obliged to steal his watch and wallet was more difficult to explain but in less enlightened times it was a standard and often successful defence.

POTTY WATCH; (US) a special watch on a person suspected of swallowing drugs and contraband.

POUND; (US) a five-year prison sentence.

POWDER, TO TAKE A; (US) to run away or absent oneself from the scene of a crime.

PRAT; 1. the buttocks. 2. the vagina 3. a fool, used as a general term of abuse.

PROBLEM; 1. a person causing serious trouble to a criminal organisation and one who is likely to be killed as a result. 2. difficulties with the authorities.

PRODUCER; the form HORT 1, issued by traffic officers requiring the production of a driving licence and insurance certificate at a police station.

PROS, THE; the prosecution.

PRO SKIRT; (US) a prostitute.

PROSS(IE) (Y): a prostitute.

PRUNO: (US) illegal prison-brewed alcohol.

PUFF: cannabis. Another of the children's songs played by the BBC without full comprehension of the words was *Puff the Magic Dragon*.

PUG: 1. (US Bl) a homosexual. 2. a boxer.

PULL: 1. arrest for questioning, usually followed by a release without charge. 2. to stop a horse from winning. 3. to attract a woman through charm or wealth, 'He can't half pull the birds.' 4. (Aus) a warning.

PULL THE TRAIN: to have consecutive sex with a number of men.

PUMP: 1. the heart, 'I shot him in the pump.' 2. to extract information.

PUMPING IRON: weightlifting.

PUNK: 1. a homosexual's catamite. 2. a young, ill-mannered upstart thief.

PUNTER: 1. a gambler. 2. a prostitute's client. 3. the target of any small-time confidence trick.

PUPPIES: (US) shoes. 'My puppies are barking' = 'My feet are hurting.'

PURPLE BOB: (US) a male person kept by a homosexual. The lavender version of a Red Bob (qv).

PUSSY: 1. the cat-o'-nine-tails. 2. a woman regarded as a sexual object, ex the pudenda. 3. a prostitute who would allow herself to be whipped. 4. Furs.

PUSSY-WHIPPED: a man subject to sexual domination by a woman.

PUT AWAY: to be sent to prison.

PUT ON ARMOUR: (US) to layer oneself with magazines to deflect knife wounds in a prison fight.

PUT ONE'S HANDS UP: to confess to a crime and/or plead guilty.

PUT OUT: to make oneself available for invariably unpaid sex, 'Does she put out?'

PUT THE HORNS ON: 1. to cuckold. 2. to try to obtain better luck in a casino by moving position or by carrying a charm such as a rabbit's foot.

PUT THE NIPS IN: (Aus) to extort.

PUT THE SCREWS ON: to extract information by intimidation, ex thumbscrews.

Q.: 1. San Quentin prison. 2. queer.

Q.E., TO GO: Queen's Evidence, evidence given by an accomplice in the hope of a lighter sentence.

Q.T.: quiet, secrecy, 'We did it on the QT.'

QUAIL: a sexually attractive woman.

QUASIMODO: the old term for a Red Band (qv) who cleaned the prison chapel, ex *The Hunchback of Notre Dame*.

QUEAN: 1. a homosexual. 2. (Scots) a young girl.

QUEEN: 1. £9. 2. a homosexual. 3. (US) a female gang member.

QUEER: 1. a homosexual. 2. suspect, worthless. 3. counterfeit money.

QUEER FELLOW: a condemned man, Brendan Behan, *The Quare Fellow*.

QUEER-HAWK: (Glas) 1. a mentally disturbed person. 2. a homosexual (rare).

QUEER QUARTET: the four officers (two on, two off) detailed to watch over a man in the death cell. They were brought from outside prisons.

QUEER STREET, TO BE IN: to be in financial difficulties, ex Carey Street, the former home of the bankruptcy court.

QUICAS: (Sp pris) a guard or policeman.

QUICK, ON THE: to steal.

QUICKY: a drink or act of coitus taken hurriedly.

QUID: 1. £1, originally one guinea. 2. a chew of tobacco.

QUIFF: 1. the vagina. 2. a prostitute. 3. sexual intercourse.

QUILL: a folded matchbox cover used for sniffing drugs.

QUIM: as quiff. Old English. In a parody of the popular song *Yes My Darling Daughter*, the girl is advised when swimming 'Don't let the boys touch your quim. Keep it under water.'

QUINCE: (Aus) a homosexual.

QUOD: old term for prison, probably first a corruption then diminution of quadrangle where prisoners were exercised.

R

RAB; a till.

RABBI; (US) 1. a senior police officer who will assist, advise and, if necessary, protect a junior officer in the early stages of his career. 2. an Underworld boss.

RABBIT BLOOD; (US) the desire to escape from prison.

RABBIT ON; 1. to talk endlessly, ex rabbit and pork = talk. 2. to run away.

RACECOURSE CHARLIE; (US) cocaine which, along with strychnine, was used to speed up slow animals.

RACKET; 1. a criminal enterprise. 2. (NYPD) a private party.

RADDIES; the Italian gangs of the 1920s and 1930s in the Clerkenwell area of London, ex Radicals.

RADICS; (WI) the police.

RADIO RENTAL; insane, ex Radio Rental = mental.

RAINBOWS; tuinal capsules.

RAIN, IT LOOKS LIKE; an arrest is imminent.

RAINY DAY WOMAN; (US) marijuana.

RAKE; (Scots) to search.

RAMMING; driving a car through a shop window to effect a theft.

RAMP; 1. a search 2. a swindle.

RAM-RAID; a smash and grab robbery involving the use of stolen high-powered cars or vans which were then driven into the windows of electrical and jewellery shops. In this, more usually Northern-based sport, the cars were often BMWs and Rovers and were loaded with paving stones and bricks which could be hurled in the path of any chasing police cars.

RANGE TENDER; (US) a prisoner who cleans the lavatories and showers.

RANK: to double cross.

RAP: (US) 1. a charge made on arrest. 2. a prison sentence. 3. to talk.

RAPPER: (US) someone pressing charges.

RAPSHEET: (US) a charge sheet.

RASPBERRY: 1. (US) a woman who trades sex for crack or money to buy crack. 2. a derogatory noise made orally but resembling breaking wind.

RASSCLAT: (Jam) a worthless person, literally an arsewipe (qv).

RATERO: (Sp pris) a sneak thief.

RAT FINK (SNITCH): (US) an informer.

RATS: (US) dice, rats and mice = dice.

RAZED: (US) under the influence of drugs.

READER: book or magazine, 'Let's have a look at your reader.'

READY-EYE, IT WAS A: caught in a trap by the police, often as a result of betrayal by a member of the team.

READY-EYED: Knowing the full position.

RED: 1. gold. (US) 2. a successful day, 'make it red'. 3. under the influence of drugs.

RED BAND: a trusted prisoner who may move about the jail, ex the armband.

RED, IN THE: to be in the money, ex red meaning gold. It is the opposite to the standard usage of meaning in debt which derives from the red ink in a bank ledger.

RED BOB: (Aus) a pimp. His possessions are said to be a toothbrush and a towel.

REDDITE: a jeweller, ex one who handles gold.

REDFEARN, TO GET OFF AT: (Aus) coitus interruptus. Redfearn is one stop short of Sydney station on the rail system.

RED LIGHT; (Aus) a senior zwarder.

RED-LIGHT DISTRICT; the brothel quarter of a town, ex the practice of hanging red lamps in windows to indicate the availability of occupants. The practice may have originated in Dodge City, Kansas when train crews left their red lamps outside brothels so they could be traced quickly in an emergency.

RED PENNY MAN; (Aus) a pimp.

RED RUM; murder, backslang.

RED SNAPPER; (US) the vagina.

REHASH; (US) a bankruptcy fraud the equivalent of a long firm fraud (qv) but one in which the fraudsman petitions for bankruptcy with a view to avoiding prosecution.

REIGN; (Aus) to be out of prison.

RESERVE GAME, THE; a form of bank robbery. In the mid-1990s it was discovered that certain banks had their reserve, averaging £40,000, delivered on a certain day and because the vault was time-locked the cash had to be kept in the chief cashier's safe. Robbers waited for the security van to leave and then entered the bank, took hold of a member of staff or customer and demanded the reserve.

RESPECT; a display of deference based on fear and particularly required in organised crime circles. Freddie Foreman, *Respect*.

RICHARD; a girlfriend, ex Richard the Third = bird.

RICHARD, TO BE IN THE; to be in trouble, ex Richard the Turd (Third) or Dick the Shit.

RICKING; acting as a shill (qv). Marilyn Wisbey, *Gangster's Moll*, 'Ricking was pretending to go [to a pavement perfume dealer] with a £5 and act like you realise it's a bargain. The public would be like sheep and follow suit.'

RICO; The Racketeer Influenced and Corrupt Organisations Act 1970 which allows prosecutors to seek higher sentences for those convicted of organised crime.

RIDE; (Irish) to rape or bugger. John Mooney, *Gangster*, 'I'm going to kidnap your son and ride him.'

RIDE DOWN; (US) a prison gang attack.

RIDE ON; a drive-by shooting.

RIDE, TAKE FOR A; to take away and kill. The dubious credit for coining the phrase goes to Earl Weiss. The victim Steve Wisniewski was lured into a car in Chicago and killed in Libertyville some 25 miles away in July 1921.

RIDING THE BROOM; 1. (US) conveying threats to female prisoners. 2. a woman prisoner who prophesies ill fortune is said to be riding the broom.

RIG; 1. (Aus) a trick or put-up job. 2. to fix, as in betting or a result. 3. a horse with only one testicle.

RIGHT; severe, 'I give him a right talking to.'

RIGHT ARM; the second ranking member or underboss of a Mafia family.

RINGER; a lookalike and so something which can be substituted for another, usually a less able horse or greyhound, and so win at a long price.

RINGERBARRY; a person who improperly returns goods to a store for a refund, ex the great 20c racecourse swindler Peter Barry who liked, after he came out of prison, to be known as the King of the Ringers. On his release he set up a horse tipping service trading on his conviction.

RING-IN; (Aus) a substitute, usually fraudulent.

RIP A NEW ASSHOLE; (US) to beat badly.

RIVER, TO BE ON THE; a heavy drinking session, River Ouse = booze.

ROAD DOG; (US gang) a close friend.

ROCKAFELLA; (US) to kill, 'rock him to sleep.'

ROCKA NIXEYS; to say nothing, ex Romany rocka = to speak and nixeys = nothing.

ROCKING; (US) a prison gang attack.

ROCKS; diamonds.

ROCKS, ON THE; to be in financial trouble, ex shipwreck.

ROD; (US) a gun.

ROFE; four years' penal servitude.

ROGER; 1. a drug habit, ex Roger Rabbit = habit 'I've caned 18 Joeys this week and now I've got a raving Roger.' 2. to have sexual intercourse.

ROGER MELLIE; television, ex the *Viz* cartoon character, Roger Mellie = telly.

ROLLED UP; (US) to be arrested.

RORTER; a confidence trickster, originally ex to rort = to fix a ballot.

RORY; cell door, ex Rory O'Moore = door.

ROSELEAF; (Aus) homosexual fellatio.

ROUNDER; (Aus and Can) 1. a criminal. 2. (US) a gang member.

ROUSTABOUT; (Aus) a general hand or labourer.

ROZZER; a police officer, poss. ex Scots, a boaster or ex Romany *roozlo* = strong. A joke recruiting slogan for the police in the 1970s was 'Rozzers rest when not arresting.'

RUBBERNECKING; watching, e.g. a game of cards or, more usually, a road accident or fire.

RUB OUT; to dispose of. In American slang it would normally mean to kill. In English prison slang it would only mean a beating.

RUG; a wig.

RUG MUNCHING; cunnilingus, particularly lesbian.

RULE 43; the former prison rule under which a prisoner e.g. a child molester or informer might apply to be segregated from the rest of the prison population.

RUMBLE; 1. a fight. 2. the news. 3. to find out the truth.

rell: bank roll
cash 141 *rough + tumble*

S

SABANA; (Sp pris) a White person.

SAFE; the vagina, a place for concealing contraband to be smuggled into prison.

SAIL; (US gang) to be released on bail.

SAND; (US) sugar.

SAND JOCKEY; an Arab.

SAN QUENTIN QUAIL; (US) a tempting looking girl under the age of consent.

SARBUT; an informer (Birmingham slang), apparently a proper name. See also Bertie.

SATELLITE; (US) a gang hanger-on.

SCAFFING; 1. using a builder's metal tube to punch out an ignition lock. 2. causing criminal damage to expensive motor cars.

SCHWARTZER; (Yiddish) a Black person.

SCOOBY; a prison officer ex Scooby Doo = screw. More common in the south of England.

SCOPE; to look over.

SCORE; 1. to buy drugs 2. to have sex with a new woman. 3. £20. 4. the complete picture, 'He knows the score.'

SCRAG ENDS; odd or damaged notes kept in every bank till which end up in a robber's bag. £10 Clydesdale notes are most prevalent.

SCRATCHING; searching for drugs.

SCREW; 1. to have sexual intercourse. 2. to disregard, 'Screw him.' 3. to burgle. 4. (US) to leave, 'Let's screw before the cops arrive.' 5. a prison guard. The term is regarded as archaic in American prison slang.

SCRIPT; a drug prescription.

142

SCRIPTWRITING; the method of presenting a police case by a complete fabrication of the evidence assigning parts to each officer who would then write up his or her notebook in accordance with the part assigned. James Morton, *Bent Coppers*, 'All officers could do it but at pretty near every police station there would be some guys who excelled at being scriptwriters.'

SCRUM DOWN; (Aus) a meeting of police officers to ensure everyone tells the same version of events in court.

SEEING TO; a beating, worse than a slap.

SELL, (UP THE RIVER); to betray, and so send a man up the river to Sing Sing prison.

SEMEN DEMON; (US pris) a passive homosexual.

SERIOUS HEADACHE; a gunshot wound to the head.

SERIOUS TROUBLE; the position of a person who has offended organised crime figures and is liable to be killed.

SET TRIPPING; (US) changing gangs.

SEVENTY-ONE; (Aus) anal intercourse.

SHADE; to obtain a narrow decision in a boxing bout.

SHADES; sunglasses.

SHAFT; 1. to swindle or steal, 'He shafted me over the goods.' 2. to have sex.

SHAG; 1. heroin. 2. to have sex.

SHAG ON A ROCK, TO BE LIKE A; (Aus) to be left high and dry.

SHAKEDOWN; 1. to search. 2. extortion, ex the person is shaken to see what he has in his pockets. 3. a cheap night's lodging, poss. ex the mattress was shaken for bugs.

SHAKES, THE; the trembling of the hands after an excess of alcohol or drugs.

SHAM; a policeman, poss. ex shamrock. There have always been a high percentage of

Irishmen who were New York and Boston officers. Another explanation is that it is short for shamus (qv). The third is that it is the Underworld's contempt for the Finest (qv) .

SHAMEZ: the police, ex Yiddish a beadle or usher in a synagogue.

SHAMUS: a private detective, ex the above.

SHANGHAI: to transfer a prisoner from one jail to another overnight. 'About four in the morning they'd come to your door, and say "You're going" and tell you to pack your gear. They wouldn't tell you where you was going until you got there.'

SHANK: a knife or other sharpened weapon.

SHANK'S MARE: (US) 1. to ride. 2. to stab.

SHARK: 1. a gambler who pretends to be less able at cards, pool etc until the stakes are sufficiently high. 2. a moneylender, abb. loan shark (qv).

SHEBEEN: an illegal drinking establishment.

SHEEP RANCH: a brothel where the girls will undertake kinky sex.

SHEET: (US) a police record.

SHEILA: 1. (Aus) a girl, ex shaler, ex the Irish female name. 2. a two-headed penny used in Two Up.

SHELF: 1. prison. 2. (Aus) to inform and therefore put in prison.

SHELL GAME: a version of the three-card trick, this time played with thimbles and a pea.

SHIESTY: crafty, untrustworthy, ex shyster (qv).

SHILL: a person run by the house who plays an otherwise empty card or dice table to draw other gamblers. Gamblers are superstitious and will not be the first at a table. The shill neither wins nor loses. The practice is illegal in Britain.

SHIRTLIFTER: a homosexual.

SHIT: heroin.

SHIT, A LOAD OF: nonsense.

SHITCAN: a case which is likely to remain unsolved by the police is put on one side or shit-canned.

SHITFACED: very drunk, poss. ex the necessity of leaning into the lavatory pan to vomit.

SHIT PARCEL DUTY: prison yard sweeping, ex prisoners throwing packets of excrement into the yard during the night because of the lack of lavatory facilities in their cells.

SHIVING: see chiving.

SHMEE: 1. (US) heroin. 2. regulations.

SHONKED, TO BE: to execute a burglary and find nothing worth stealing.

SHONUS: (US) a detective.

SHOOTER: 1. a gun. 2. a person who holds the drugs on the street before handing them to the buyer.

SHOOTING GALLERY: a place where addicts congregate to shoot up.

SHOOT UP: to inject intravenously.

SHOP: to inform.

SHORT EYES: a child molester.

SHOULDER SURFING: standing at a cash till and stealing the credit card from the withdrawer.

SHOVEL: prison, ex shovel and pick = nick.

SHYLOCK: a moneylender, ex Shakespeare.

SHYSTER: a crooked lawyer, now lawyers generally, poss. ex Eugene Scheuster, an Essex Market, New York lawyer of the 1850s.

SICILIAN NECKTIE: wire tied around the neck as a garrotte.

SIGN ON YOUR BACK, TO HAVE A: to be a known crooked gambler.

SIMCHA: (Yiddish) a pimp.

SIX AND EIGHT: a non criminal, six and eight = straight.

SKANK: 1. a highly potent and addictive form of cannabis. 2. a promiscuous or unclean female.

SKANKY HOE: a promiscuous or unclean female, ex skanky whore.

SKELL: (US police) a criminal.

SKETCH: to act excessively nervously, especially whilst on marijuana.

SKETELL: a promiscuous woman.

SKID AROUND: to be of easy virtue, 'She skids around a lot.'

SKID ARTIST: a getaway driver.

SKID ROW: (US) a run down area populated by the homeless, ex loggers' slang. Skid road was a greased corduroy track of saplings on which logs were skidded to the river to be floated to saw mills. c. 1900 to skid the road = to be a tramp or hobo.

SKIDS, TO PUT THE S. UNDER:

to inform to the police. W.R. Burnett, *Little Caesar*.

SKIM: to take a slice of an employer's profits particularly from a casino.

SKIMMING UP: smoking cannabis.

SKIN: (US) a shirt.

SKIN GAME: a confidence trick. The trickster would have the shirt from the back of his victim.

SKINK: (Bl) a White person, a term of abuse.

SKINT: penniless, boracic lint = skint.

SKIN WORKER: a thief who specialises in stealing furs.

SKIPPERING: sleeping rough, travelling with one's belongings.

SKO: abb. of skanky hoe (qv).

SKY: a pocket, sky rocket = pocket.

SKY PILOT: a clergyman.

SLABBED AND SLID: an

ex-inmate no longer recalled with clarity by those still inside prison.

SLAG; an elderly, worn out prostitute, now in more general use for a woman who hands out sexual favours indiscriminately.

SLAM AND JAM; (US) a violent form of arrest.

SLAMMER; prison, ex the noise of the steel cell shutting. It is said that no one who has not served a sentence can fully understand the haunting reality of the slamming at night.

SLANG; to deal in drugs, 'He's loaded because he's slanging.'

SLAPPER; a young girl of poor morals.

SLAPPERAT; a woman who will accept a whipping as part of sex. One such was one of the victims of Neville Heath.

SLASH; 1. the vagina. 2. to urinate.

SLASH JOB; (US) self-mutilation in prison.

SLAUGHTER; 1. the temporary hiding place for stolen goods. 2. to defeat comprehensively either physically or e.g. in cross-examination.

SLAUGHTERHOUSE; a low-quality brothel, the end of the line for the inmates.

SLAVE; (US) female gang member.

SLEEP; 1. (UK) a sentence of three years. 2. (US) a sentence of one year.

SLEEVED; (US) an arm covered in tattoos.

SLEEVES; cartons of smuggled cigarettes.

SLEIGH RIDE; cocaine.

SLICE OF THE ACTION; a portion of the profits from a crime family's business.

SLINGING INK; (US) prison tattooing.

SLINGING TROUT; (US) throwing excreta at prison guards.

SLOP: (Scots) a policeman, ex esclop.

SLOPPING OUT: emptying chamber pots in prison before breakfast. The practice officially ceased on 12 April 1996.

SLOSH: 1. coffee stall 2. to hit.

SLOT: (Aus) a prison.

SLUSH: counterfeit money.

SLUSH FUND: money set aside for bribery.

SMACK: 1. heroin. 2. a bad beating but not one in which limbs are broken.

SMASH: loose change or money.

SMOGGED, TO BE: to die in the gas chamber.

SMOKE: opium.

SMOKE, THE: London, ex the one-time fogs.

SMOTHER: 1. a mask or disguise used when committing robbery etc. 2. an overcoat.

SMOTHER GAME: pickpocketing with the use of a coat.

SMURFING: a relatively unsophisticated form of money laundering in which amounts of less than £10,000, or in the United States $10,000 are paid into accounts held by relatives and friends and as such do not require the bank to report the investment to the authorities.

SMUTTER: (Yiddish) imitation.

SMUTTER GAME: taking photographs of tourists without a film in the camera. They pay a deposit on the photograph to be developed later.

SNATCH: the vagina.

SNIDE: 1. crooked, imitation. 2. an unpleasant remark.

SNIDE SHOOTER: an imitation firearm.

SNIPE: (US pris) a re-usable cigarette butt.

SNITCH: 1. to inform. 2. an informer.

SNOUT; 1. tobacco, ex the practice when silence was required in prison of putting a finger to the side of the nose. 2. an informer.

SNOW; 1. cocaine, ex its appearance, occ. morphine. 2. (UK) silver coins or articles.

SNOW CONE; an ice pick.

SNOWDROPPING; stealing women's underwear usually from a clothesline, ex the days when all underwear was white.

SNOWDROPS; the American military police, ex the colour of their caps.

SNOW JOB; an uninformative, worthless report.

SNUFF; to die, ex snuffing a candle.

SNUFF MOVIE; a pornographic film in which the victim, very often a child who has been tortured, is apparently, and in real life may have been, killed at the end.

SOAK; to obtain a considerable amount of money from a victim.

SOLDIER; the lowest rank of made men in the Mafia.

SORT OUT; 1. to intimidate or bribe a witness. 2. to beat up.

SOUP; 1. nitroglycerine, made by simmering dynamite very gently in water. 2. a watch.

SOUTHIE; South Boston, home of the so-called Irish mafia.

SPACE BLANKET; a foil sheet used for burglary. Once draped over the burglar it does not register body heat or movement and so will not set off alarms.

SPANISH PRISONER SWINDLE; a confidence trick dating from 17c, in which the victim is persuaded to send money to a prisoner of war or refugee in return for a mythical share of stolen money.

SPANK; to beat up.

SPANKED, TO BE; (US) to be intoxicated.

SPARE; a woman available for extra-marital intercourse.

SPARE, TO GO; to be extremely angry.

SPARKLERS; diamonds.

SPARSIE; sixpence.

SPEED; amphetamines.

SPEEDBALL; a cocaine and heroin injection.

SPIELER; an illegal gambling club, ex the German.

SPIV; a person who dresses flashily and lives from minor crime, poss. ex the reverse of Very Important Persons (VIPs) or Suspected persons and itinerant vagrants, poss. ex Romany, *spivic*, a word of contempt for someone who picks up another's leavings.

SPLIT; 1. to inform or turn Queen's Evidence. 2. to run away. 3. to share profits. 4. to sever connections. 5. a policeman.

SPLIT BEAVER; (US) the female pudenda.

SPONDULIX; money.

SPONSOR; (US) a man who sends money to a woman in prison. In general he will not have known her before.

SPOTTER; a detective. The term derives from the practice employed by the Pinkerton Detective Agency of ensuring that as many of their operatives as possible saw any criminal visiting the agency. Detailed descriptions of them were then prepared and circulated.

SPRATT; sixpence.

SPRAZZY; sixpence.

SPRING; to organise a prison escape.

SPRUCE; to lie.

SQUAT SEAT; the electric chair.

SQUEAL; to inform, ex the noise of a pig and also noise made when the pig was stolen.

SQUEALER; 1. someone who cannot be trusted. 2. a police radio car. 3. (Aus) a young girl, cf grunter.

SQUEEZE: (US) 1. a girlfriend. 2. (US BI) PCP mixed with embalming fluid. 3. a drug connection.

STABLE: 1. (US BI) the group of prostitutes working for one pimp. 2. a group of boxers or entertainers under one manager.

STAG, TO TURN: to inform.

STAINED WITNESS: (HK) one who gives evidence against a gang leader and so is stained or marked for death.

STAIR JUMPING: stealing from offices, poss. ex the need to escape at speed.

STAIRS, TO BE SENT UP THE: to be sent for sentence at the Crown Court.

STALL: to delay.

STALLION: (US BI) a tall, good-looking woman.

STANDOVER: (Aus) robbery.

STANDOVER MAN: (Aus) a robber. Standover men in Australia have been particularly vicious and are quite willing to prey on other crooks who have made a successful haul. In the 1960s one particular group which operated with considerable success was known as the Toecutters (qv).

STAND-UP GUY: (US) one who will not inform on his colleagues and so forfeits more favourable treatment for himself.

STAR: 1. a first-time prisoner. 2. a pimp's most successful prostitute.

STARBURSTS: another form of money laundering similar in execution to strings (qv). Funds are layered through shell companies and nominees before being reintegrated in the form of properties.

STARDUST: cocaine.

STASH: a cache of drugs.

STAUNCH: a witness who will not bow to pressure to change his or her evidence.

STEAMER: 1. a victim of a trick or an easy touch, steam tug = mug. 2. a horse whose starting price dramatically shortens before the race. 3. a member of a gang of robbers.

STEAMING: mass robbery of e.g. passengers on a train or stallholders at a market.

STENDER: a villain from the East End.

STEW: (Aus) a fixed horse race or sporting event.

STICKMAN: the operator of a cheating device at a carnival or fairground.

STICKSING: (WI) pickpocketing.

STICKS MEN: (WI) pickpockets, ex 'five, six pick up sticks'.

STIFF: 1. a corpse. 2. a letter smuggled from prison.

STILLSONS: boltcutters which could be concealed in the sleeve, ex the manufacturer.

STING: a confidence trick.

STIR: prison, either ex Joe Gurr = stir or the Romany *sturiben* meaning to confine.

STIRVILLE: Sing Sing prison.

STONE: an extreme, e.g. rich or poor.

STONE KILLER: (US) efficient and ruthless professional killer.

STONES: 1. jewels. 2. testicles.

STONK: to hurl abuse.

STOOL (PIGEON): an informer, ex a pigeon fastened to a stool as a decoy.

STRAIGHT: 1. a non-criminal. 2. Goods which are not stolen, 'they're straight'. 3. heterosexual.

STRAIGHTEN OUT: to deal with e.g. a loan defaulter.

STRAIGHTENED OUT: to be inducted into the Mafia.

STRAIGHTENER: a fistfight at the end of which the quarrel will be deemed to be resolved.

STRAIGHT-GOER: a non-criminal.

STRAP: to carry a gun.

STRAPPED, TO BE; to be without, 'I'm strapped for cash.'

STREAKING; running naked across the field at a sporting event. The first recorded case was in April 1974 at Twickenham. Later a woman, ran bare-breasted to great acclaim. She became a minor celebrity and was later invited to take part in a charity match billed as Rugby's favourite hooker.

STRING; 1. the women working for one pimp. 2. a method of hiding illicit funds in offshore accounts, often through a series of nominees.

STRINGS; a method of laundering money.

STRIPE; 1. £1. 2. to cut. The cutting was often done across the buttocks. It was said that Billy Hill, the Gangleader of the 1950s, paid £1 per stitch.

STRUMMING; masturbation.

STUFFER AND SWALLOWER; a drug courier who hides the drugs in his or her vagina or anus.

STUMER; 1. a mistake. 2. a cheque or bank draft which is worthless to a burglar.

SUGAR; 1. a term of endearment but often said to a man who is paying for his pleasure. 2. bribe money. 3. narcotics. 4. (euph) shit, 'Well . . . sugar.'

SUGAR PIMP; one who uses charm rather than violence to obtain co-operation from his string.

SUITCASE; (US pris) the anus.

SUITCASING; concealing drugs in the anus or vagina.

SUKI; (Russ) a turncoat, scab. Lit. bitch.

SURFING; riding between two carriages on the London underground.

SURI; (Jap) a pickpocket, ex *suritsukeru*, literally rubbing against.

SUS; a suspected person. Under the Vagrancy Act a person could be convicted of two apparently unsuccessful

stripped; broke

attempts to steal, e.g. trying car door handles. Later it was used extensively against Black youths thought to be pickpockets. Under the Act a police officer could also arrest a person for being a 'known or reputed thief suspected of ...'. The offence was abolished by the Larceny Act 1975.

SUZY WONG; (HK) a Chinese woman who seeks out western men usually for financial reasons, ex Richard Mason, *The World of Suzy Wong*.

SWAG; 1. stolen goods. 2. to arrest. 'They swagged me down the peter over some smutter tom.'

SWANK; stolen goods.

SWAPPING SPIT; (US) 1. two men kissing. 2. male oral sex.

SWEEDY; the derisory name given to regional officers investigating corruption by Metropolitan Police officers during Operation Countryman in the 1960s. The investigation was less than a complete success.

SWEENEY; the Flying Squad, ex either Sweeney Todd = Flying Squad or the name of a former senior detective.

SWEET; amenable to bribery, 'He's sweet (as a nut).'

SWEETENER; a bribe or additional payment such as an illegal cash top up on a lawyer's legal aid fees.

SWEETMAN; (WI) a pimp.

SWEETS; amphetamines.

SWIFT; knowingly to make a false arrest.

SWING; to be hanged.

SWING FOR; to die , ex 'I'll swing for him' = 'I don't mind being hanged because I'm going to kill him.'

SWINGING THE LINE; the practice of passing books, tobacco or messages from one cell to another by means of a line, usually obtained from the mailbag shop.

SWING THE TYPEWRITER; to make a statement to the police.

SWITCH; a sauna where the client can massage the girl.

SWITCHBLADE; (US) a flick knife. The blade springs open when a button is pressed on the handle.

SWITCHHITTER; bi-sexual, ex the ability of a baseball player to bat right-and left-handed.

SWOON; to lose a contest deliberately.

SWORDSMAN; 1. a receiver of stolen property. 2. a successful sexually active man.

SWY; (Aus) a two-year prison sentence, prob. ex the German Zwei.

T

T; marijuana.

TAB; 1. the ear. 2. an Ecstasy tablet. 3. (US) written note passed from one prisoner to another.

TABLE, UNDER THE; 1. dishonestly. 2. drunk.

TABS, TO KEEP T. ON; to follow progress, to watch.

TACS; (US pris) tattoos.

TAFFIA, THE; Welsh criminals, often in Dartmoor prison.

TAG; 1. (US) an arrest warrant. 2. the signature of a graffiti writer.

TAIL; 1. the female genitals. 2. women in the sexual sense, 'I had some tail last night.' *The Taming of the Shrew*, Petruchio: 'What with my tongue in your tail? Nay, come again. Good Kate, I am a Gentleman.' (US) 3. a reward. 4. the buttocks. 5. to follow.

TAILGATE; to drive danger-ously close to another vehicle.

TAILOR MADE; machine-made cigarette as opposed to hand-rolled tobacco, ex a bespoke suit.

TAKE; 1. a share of proceeds of crime. 2. to execute a crime, 'We can take the bank on Friday.'

TAKE A BAND; to take drugs.

TAKE A BATH; to lose all one's money, prob. by a trick or swin-dle, ex the Yiddish *Er haut mikh gefirt in bod arayn* when at the turn of the century immigrants had to be tricked into taking off their clothes to go to a bath-house for decontamination.

TAKE A FALL; (US) to be arrested or sent to prison, ex wrestling.

TAKE A POWDER; to desert or run away.

TAKE, ON THE; a police officer or prison warder susceptible to bribery.

TAKE TO THE CLEANERS: to win all one's opponent's money, poss. by swindling.

TALENT: 1. a good-looking girl. 2. (US) a successful thief at a carnival.

TALK: to confess or inform.

TALK CABBAGE: (police) to co-operate with officers from another force with no reserve on either side.

TALK TURKEY: (US) to speak frankly.

TANK: 1. a prison cell. 2. to drink to excess, as in 'tanked up'.

TANK, TO GO IN THE: to lose a boxing bout deliberately, usually for betting purposes but possibly to assist the career of an opponent.

TAP CITY, TO BE IN: (US) to have no money, ex to tap, to borrow.

TAPE: to size up.

TATS: (US pris) tattoos.

TEA: marijuana.

TEAHEAD: a user of cannabis.

TEALEAF: a thief.

TEAM: gang.

TEA ROOM: (US) a meeting place e.g. lavatory for homosexuals, cf cottage. Laud Humphreys, *The Tea Room Trade*.

TEAR UP: a fight.

"TEC: a detective.

TECATA: heroin.

TELEPHONE NUMBERS: an excessively high figure demanded as payment, 'He's talking telephone numbers.'

TELL THE TALE: to work a confidence trick, particularly on a racecourse, explaining how a horse cannot lose.

TENDERLOIN: a district where there is the opportunity for bribery and corruption. The original tenderloin was the old 29th precinct in New York City which included Times Square, ex the succulent cut of meat.

TERRORDOME; Attica prison, New York State.

THATCHERVILLES; the cardboard cities of homeless which proliferated in London during the premiership of Margaret Thatcher, ex Hoovervilles, the hobo jungles of the American Depression and cf the French, Bidonvilles, iron shanty towns.

THE DEUCE; (US) 42nd St, New York between Sixth and Ninth avenues.

THE GERMANS; (Liverpool) prison officers.

THIEVES' PONCE; a criminal who takes money from the efforts of others as a form of taxation rather than earning himself. Both the 1950s gang leader Jack Spot and the Kray Twins were regarded as thieves'ponces.

THIN AND THICK; the penis, thin and thick = prick.

THREADS; clothing.

THREE-CARD MONTE; (US) the American name for Find the Lady (qv). It has little to do with monte, the Mexican gambling game.

THREE UP; the practice of putting three men in a cell designed for two. Originally done to eliminate the temptations of homosexuality it is now, more prosaically, because of overcrowding.

THROW; to lose deliberately, usually for betting purposes. One of the best-known examples is the loss of the 1919 World Series by the Chicago White Sox, known afterwards as the Black Sox.

THROWAWAY; a shirt or jacket thrown away by a mugger to confuse any pursuers.

THROWDOWN; (US) 1. a weapon dropped by police at the scene of a shooting to justify the killing of an unarmed suspect. 2. A fight.

THROW THE BOOK AT; to sentence heavily.

THROW THE BOOK AWAY; (US)

to conduct a court case without reference to due process of law.

THROW THE KEY AWAY: to sentence heavily.

THUMPER: (US gang) a gun.

TICKET: an MOT certificate.

TICKLE: 1. an unexpected and, from the viewpoint of the police, fortuitous arrest. 2. money obtained by betting or a successful theft or con trick.

TICKLER: the cat-o'-nine-tails. Flogging was abolished in 1948.

TIDY-UP: (Aus) 1. to deal with comprehensively. 2. police questioning.

TIGER CAGE: (US pris) the underground security section where many Mafiosi and other major criminals are now held.

TILBURY DOCKER: a defaulter, ex Tilbury docker = locker.

TIME: any prison sentence, ex bird-lime = time. One chairman of Quarter Sessions is said to have remarked to a prisoner who stole a clock, 'If it's time you want, I'll give you three months.'

TIME, HAVE YOU GOT THE: traditional inquiry by prospective clients of street prostitutes. The reply was supposed to be, 'Yes, if you've got the money.'

TIMOTHY: (Aus) a brothel, common since 1950s but of unknown origin.

TIN: 1. money. 2. (US) a policeman's badge.

TINA: abb. of Christina, crystal methamphetamine.

TINKLE: to urinate, 'There's many a man likes to watch a girl tinkle.'

TIP: (US) a gang.

TIP OFF: the warning of an impending disaster such as a police raid.

TIPPED UP: (US pris) gang affiliated.

TISH: (US) money in a prostitute's stocking. A trick played on girls was to push a wad of folded paper into the stocking top. It would turn out to be tissue paper.

TITHEAD: a policeman, ex the shape of the helmet. Once a common chant at football matches.

TNUC: a fool, backslang.

TOBY: a police division.

TOD, TO BE ON ONE'S: ex Tod Sloan = alone. Sloan was a talented but crooked American jockey who revolutionised the riding of racehorses in England at the beginning of 20c. He was eventually deported as an undesirable alien.

TOECUTTERS: a particularly violent gang of Australian robbers who preyed on other gangs, threatening them with amputation if they did not share the profits.

TOE IT: to accelerate rapidly, 'The bend was coming up so I toed it.'

TOERAG: an undesirable or worthless person, ex the bandages worn on the feet of beggars.

TOKE: 1. bread. 2. a homemade cigarette.

TOM: 1. a prostitute, ex tomboy, a mannish prostitute. 2. jewellery, ex tomfoolery. 3. an injection of a narcotic, Tom Mix = fix.

TOM AND DICK: vomiting, Tom and Dick = sick.

TOMATO CAN: a boxer put in the ring with no hope of winning but who is on the bill simply to make up numbers.

TOMMERS: a jewellery shop.

TOMMY GUN: the Thompson machine gun highly favoured in Chicago in the liquor wars of the 1920s.

TOM SQUAD: the Vice Squad.

TOM TIT: to defecate, tom it = shit.

TON: 1. £100. 2. 100 mph.

TON UP BOY: one whose car or motorbike could reach 100 mph.

tomato: attractive woman

TOOL; 1. a weapon or house-breaking equipment. 2. the penis. 3. a dupe. 4. a catamite.

TOOLED-UP; (US) carrying weapons.

TOOT; money.

TOOT A LINE; to sniff cocaine.

TOP ONESELF; to commit suicide.

TORCH; a person who commits arson, usually for insurance purposes.

TORCH, TO CARRY A; unrequited love, often of a prostitute for her pimp.

TORPEDO A DRUM; to execute a housebreaking.

TOSS; to search, 'We can toss his drum.'

TOSSER; a fool or worthless person, someone who has masturbated so much he has ruined his head.

TOSS OFF; 1. to masturbate. 2. (US gang) a girl used for sex.

TOTTER; 1. a rag and bone man. 2. a motorist whose penalty points endorsed on his licence now leave him liable for disqualification.

TOTTIE; a girl, not a prostitute, available for sexual intercourse.

TOUCH; 1. money obtained successfully and slightly dishonestly by gambling or borrowing. 2. an unexpected acquittal.

TOUCHED; 1. mentally disturbed. 2. Arrested, ex the touch on the arm by a detective.

TOUCHING THE DOG'S ARSE; (UK) Taking and driving away a motor vehicle. S. London slang, ex the initials.

TOUCH OF THE SECONDS; a change of mind (second thoughts) often about a potential criminal enterprise.

TRACKS; marks left on an arm by the use of a hypodermic needle.

TRACKS, TO MAKE; (US) to leave, ex railroad.

TRAMP'S LAGGING; three

months. Considered severe since a tramp would normally receive only a week or two.

TRAPS: (Aus) police.

TREE JUMPER: (US pris) an inmate sentenced for rape.

TRICK: 1. the sex act. 2. a prostitute's client. The implication is that the prostitute is tricking the man by taking money for something for which he should have no need to pay. 3. a period of demanding or hard work, ex 'I've done seven tricks since lunchtime.' 4. to inform.

TRICK PAD: a prostitute's place of business as opposed to her home.

TRIFECTA: (Aus) a false arrest with three charges, offensive behaviour, resisting arrest and assaulting an officer, ex a rolled-up bet.

TRIP, TO TAKE A: to experience the effects of LSD.

TRIP FOR BISCUITS, A: (US) to achieve nothing, a waste of time.

TROD: stolen goods, poss. ex trodden on and bent or poss. as from to tread, 'it didn't just walk off'. WI usage but common in South of England.

TROT: (Aus) 1. a run of luck good or bad. 2. a sequence of throws in Two Up.

TROTS: (Aus) diarrhoea.

TRUE BILL: a correct allegation, ex the bill literally handed down by a Grand Jury to determine whether a defendant should stand trial. The practice is now obsolete in Britain but still to be found in a number of American States.

TRUNK MUSIC: (US) after a victim is killed and left in the boot of a car the resulting sounds from the rotting flesh are known as trunk music.

TRUSTY: a prisoner trusted by the authorities and therefore allowed certain freedoms within a prison. In New York State prisons the use was uncommon. Outside man was the preferred expression.

TUKEY BOY: (UK BI) a gullible youth.

TUMBLE: 1. a drink. 2. to understand. 3. to have sexual intercourse.

TUMBLE, TO GIVE IT A: to try, to experiment, cf whirl.

TUMBLED, TO BE: to be found out or arrested.

TUNE UP: to hurt, 'I tuned him up.'

TUNNEL: to swindle or defraud.

TURBAN: (US) to hit on the back of the head leaving an open wound which needs bandaging, 'Give him a turban.'

TURF: territory occupied by a street gang.

TURK, TO GO: (Irish) to turn State's evidence.

TURN A TRICK: 1. to commit an act of prostitution. 2. to commit a crime.

TURN IN: to inform on somebody.

TURN ON: 1. to smoke a marijuana cigarette or to give a non-addict his first shot. 2. to excite sexually.

TURN OVER: 1. to search. 2. to cheat or rob. 3. to beat up.

TURQUOISE: a prostitute who practises anal intercourse, ex Turk ways, a reference to the alleged enthusiasm of Turkish men for this practice.

TURTLES: gloves, turtle doves = gloves.

TWEEDLE: jewellery.

TWEEDLE ON THE (TWEEDLING): 1. stealing jewellery by substituting worthless items. 2. passing off inferior goods, e.g. perfume, as genuine.

TWENTY-TWO FIFTY MAN: (US) an informer. In the 1920s the NYPD was said to have paid $22.50 as a weekly wage to informers.

TWIRL: prison officer, ex the days when keys were carried on a ring.

TWIRLS: keys, often skeleton keys.

TWIST: (Aus) a woman, ex twist and twirl = girl.

TWO AND EIGHT: nervous, two and eight = state.

TWO'D UP: two prisoners in a cell designed for one.

TWO'S UP: to share, 'Two's up on your fag?'

TWO UP: a highly popular and illegal gambling game very popular in Australia in which betting is on which number of times a coin falls heads or tails. At one time played in country and particularly mining districts in Britain, it has produced a language of its own.

U

UMBRELLA BRIGADE: Special Branch, ex their mode of dress.

UNCLE: 1. a receiver of stolen goods, sometimes a pawnbroker. The two professions often work hand in hand. 2. (US) the police. 3. a police informer.

UNCLE MILTIE: (US) crack cocaine.

UNCLE SUGAR: the FBI.

UNDERBOSS: the second highest ranking member of a Mafia family.

UNDER GLASS: in prison.

UNDER THE TONGUE: the common method of passing drugs to a prisoner by a visiting girlfriend.

UNDERWORLD: the world of organised crime.

UNPAID SHILL: casino term for a small better.

UP FRONT: money required in advance before the payee will take any action, e.g. a lawyer's fees.

UPPER AND DOWNER: railway police term for an adult and juvenile arrested together. One must go to the adult court and the other to the juvenile court.

UPPERS AND DOWNERS: amphetamines and barbiturates, stimulants and depressants.

UP THE RIVER, TO BE SENT: to go to prison, ex Ossining (Sing Sing) on the Hudson River.

UP THE STEPS: to be committed for sentence at the crown court, ex the dock had to be entered up a flight of stairs from the cells.

URGER: a member of a three-card trick team.

USER: a drug taker.

USI: unlawful sexual intercourse with a girl under 16. Once a common offence it is now much more rarely prosecuted.

165

unload
up your-alley

V

VEGA: (US) a cigar wrapping refilled with marijuana.

VEGETABLE PATCH: the communal seating by the prison wing television where hobbits watch soap-operas.

VERAS: rolling paper for tobacco, ex the singer Vera Lynn = skin.

VERBALS: oral statements of admission by a suspect which in the absence of other evidence was often sufficient to obtain a conviction, e.g. 'I only did it for the wife and kids.' These were often invented by the police. The practice was discredited in the 1980s.

VIGORISH (VIG): 1. the interest paid to a moneylender. Very often the rate will be 6 for 5, that is £6 for a week's loan of £5. A skilful loan shark can ensure that the nut (qv) is never repaid. 2. the percentage earned by a casino. 3. vigilante, by no means common in Britain but, in the form of private street patrols, likely to make an impact.

VILLAIN: police term for a local hooligan.

VILLE, THE: HMP Pentonville, London.

VIPER MAD: addicted to marijuana.

VISITING FIREMAN: free-spending visitor from out of town, e.g. a police officer who has to be entertained by a member of another force when he is sent to collect a prisoner etc. Often the fireman will have been given a list of addresses of women willing to provide sexual favours in return for a night on the town.

VOLUNTEER: a young male prostitute.

W

WACKY-BACKY; cannabis.

WALK-INS; entering business premises during working hours to steal.

WANNABEE; a would-be gang member or hanger-on.

WAREHOUSE; prison.

WASH, AT THE; stealing from washrooms in hotels, airports etc. One of the greatest of these thefts came in 1909 when, in a highly organised theft and with another man helping his escape, Herbert Grimshaw, the former jockey, stole jewels from a jeweller in the wash room of the Café Monico in Regent Street. The jeweller had been followed for days and this was noticed to be the only time he let go of his bag. Most thefts at the wash are more opportunistic.

WASTE; 1. to kill. 2. to get high on drugs. 3. to pass out.

WATER, OUT IN THE; (US) in debt.

WEAKHEART; (WI) police, derisory.

WEAK SISTER; a feeble person, a weak link.

WEDGE; a large amount of banknotes folded in half.

WEED; 1. tobacco. 2. cannabis.

WEEDING; stealing from an employer or at the scene where a crime has already been committed.

WEIGHED OFF; sentenced.

WELSH; to fail to pay a debt.

WELSHER; a dishonest book-maker on a racetrack. He welshes on paying the winning bets.

WHACK; 1. (US) a gangland execution. 2. (US) to beat up. 3. a share of profits.

WHALE; to beat badly.

WHEELMAN; the driver of a getaway car.

WHIP: a collection for a criminal in trouble or one newly released from prison.

WHIPPY: (Aus) money stolen by the police.

WHISTLE: suit, ex whistle and flute.

WHISTLE, TO BLOW THE W. ON: to give information leading to arrest or exposure. When, in an effort to stamp out possible misbehaviour in a Northern police force, a hot line was set up, there were no calls except whistles of derision, a message, 'Hitler and Ceaucescu tried this too' and a civilian member of staff who wanted to know what she had to do to get herself harassed. *News of the World*, December 1992.

WHITE: 1. £5, ex the colour of the old £5 note. 2. platinum. 3. heroin.

WHITE BALL: crack cocaine.

WHITE BOY: heroin.

WHITE BREAD: 1. (BI) a White person. 2. (Aus) a sanitary towel,

'I'm out of white bread and George is calling tonight' = 'My period is due and I need to purchase tampons.'

WHITE CROSS: amphetamine.

WHITE DUST: LSD.

WHITE GHOST: crack cocaine.

WHITE GIRL: cocaine, heroin.

WHITE-HAIRED LADY: marjuana.

WHITE HORSE: cocaine.

WHITE JUNK: heroin.

WHITE LIGHTNING: LSD.

WHIZZ, AT THE: pickpocketing, 'He's been at the whizz for years.'

WICK: the penis, 'He gets on my wick', ex Hampton Wick = prick.

WIDE: experienced, cunning. The term wide boy, very popular in the 1940s and 1950s, has now become almost obsolete.

WILAS: (US) a note smuggled from prison by a gang member with instructions for work to be undertaken outside the jail.

WILDING; gang rape.

WILLIE; (UK) 1. the penis. 2. (Aus) a wallet, 'to touch a willie' = to steal a wallet. 3. a pocket. 4. a fit.

WIND, IN THE; (US) 1. to be released on expiration of a sentence or on parole. 2. the status of a person who has left the Witness Protection Programme.

WINDOW'S OPEN, THE; inept cheating at cards or dice.

WINDOW WARRIOR; a prisoner who repeatedly shouts through his cell window.

WIRED; 1. to be carrying a concealed tape recorder. 2. to be under the influence of methamphetamines.

WOOD; hangers on and kibitzers in a casino.

WOOD, CHARLIE (MR); a police officer's truncheon, 'Here's my friend Charlie Wood.'

WOPPITZER; a kibitzer with body odour.

WORD UP; (US Bl) the truth.

WORKING GIRL; a prostitute.

WRAP-UP; 1. a robbery in which the victims are tied up. 2. to quit or retire.

WRONG; untrustworthy, esp a police informer, 'I never thought he'd turn out to be a wrong 'un.'

X

X: 1. ten dollars. 2. the control of all gambling in a district, 'The Irish have the X in the Bronx.' 3. The drug ecstasy.

XX: twenty dollars.

Y

YAHOO; 1. a vicious person, ex Jonathan Swift, *Gulliver's Travels*. 2. crack cocaine.

YAKUZA; Japanese organised crime gangs.

YALE; crack cocaine.

YANCING; sexual intercourse, ex Yiddish.

YAP; 1. a fool or dupe. 2. a farmer. 3. a petty swindler. 4. to talk foolishly or tell a tale. 5. the mouth, 'Shut your yap.'

YARD; (US) 1. a 100-year sentence. 2. 1,000 but now devalued to 100. Used principally in monetary terms. 3. a prison's recreation area. (WI) 4. home. 5. a flat or house. 6. Jamaica. (UK) 7. one hundred or any large number generally. Although usually referring to money it is also used by ticket touts left with more than they can sell, 'Anyone want a ticket? I've got a yard left.' 8. Scotland Yard.

YARD BIRD; (US) 1. a prisoner. 2. fried chicken served in prison.

YARDIE; a member of a West Indian crime group.

YARRA; (Aus) mental, ex the psychiatric hospital at Yarra Bend, Melbourne.

YAYOO; crack cocaine.

YEAR; a dollar bill.

YEGG; 1. a safecracker, poss. ex John Yegg, the first safebreaker to use nitroglycerine; poss. ex German *Jaeger* = hunter. Now often a term of derision. 2. A professional killer used by the Tongs in their wars. 3. A travelling burglar who moves from city to city.

YELLOW; 1. cowardly. 2. LSD.

YELLOW BULLETS; depressants.

YELLOW DIMPLES; LSD.

YELLOW PERIL; vegetable soup served in prison.

YELLOW STUFF; gold coins, usually counterfeit.

YELLOW SUBMARINE: marijuana, ex the song by The Beatles.

YENTZER: (Yiddish) a racketeer, cheat.

YO: (Bl) a term of greeting.

YOB: boy, backslang.

YOCKER: a foolish person or bumpkin, ex the Yiddish *Yockele*, a non-Jewish person.

YODEL: cunnilingus.

YOG: a gun, ex Romany.

YOKE: (US) to cut a throat from behind.

YOP: (Scots) to inform.

YOU KNOW HOW IT IS . . . : vague explanation when no proper excuse comes to mind.

YUBITSUME: (Jap) the practice of cutting off the top of the little finger as a gesture of apology to an oyabun (qv).

Z

Z; (US) a home-made firearm, see zip.

ZACK; (US) a prison informant.

ZANAX; (US) valium.

ZAP; to kill, often by machine gun.

ZEN; LSD.

ZIFF; a juvenile thief.

ZILCH; nothing.

ZING; to bet heavily, particularly at dice, and to play up one's winnings.

ZIP; (US) 1. an old Sicilian Mafiosi in the early part of 20c. 2. (pris) a home-made firearm, generally a short pipe 2-10 inches long. A bullet is put in the pipe and fired when a pointed steel rod is inserted and discharged by a blow of the hand rather as a ball is launched in a pinball machine. 3. cocaine.

ZIP TOP; (US) street slang for a Jewish person.

ZOL; a marijuana cigarette.

ZOMBIE; 1. a drug taker. 2. a gambler who shows no emotion when either winning or losing. 3. a horse which runs indifferently. 4. a policewoman. 5. a particularly unpleasant prison officer, one more dead than alive.

ZOO; prison generally, ex the prison at Kalamazoo, Mich.

ZOOK; (US) a worn-out prostitute.

ZOOM; 1. marijuana laced with PCP. 2. to obtain something for nothing.

ZOOT SUIT; an extreme type of dress with a drape-shaped jacket and heavily padded shoulders and tapered trousers favoured by Hispanics. The so-called zoot suit anti-Mexican riots took place in Los Angeles in the 1940s.

ZOO ZOOS: (US) sweets bought in prison shops.

ZOTZ: (US) to kill.

ZUCH: (US) an informer.

ZUCK: (US) a prison informant.

ZULU: bogus crack.

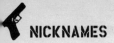

NICKNAMES

ACTION
William Jackson, 300 lb Chicago enforcer tortured to death by being hanged on a meathook.

BATH-HOUSE
John Coughlin, corrupt Chicago politician and associate of Capone, from his earlier career as a masseur.

BATTERS
Tony Arcado. That was his function working for Al Capone.

BATTLES
(UK) Alberto 'Bert' Rossi, Billy Hill associate, from his fights as a young man.

BIG TUNA
Tony Arcado, because of a fish he caught of which he was inordinately proud.

BILLY THE KID
William Bonney.

BIRDMAN OF ALCATRAZ
Robert Franklin Stroud. During his life sentences from which he was never released he became a world renowned expert on birds.

BLACK WIDOW
East Ender, Linda Calvey whose husband was killed by the police and who in turn killed her former lover. Worldwide there have been any number of Black Widows, women whose men friends have died early. They include Fay Sadler who was associated with Tommy Smithson and Jack Rosa in London.

BLACKIE
James Licavoli, the Cleveland crime boss known for his dark complexion. Curiously one of his aliases was Jimmy White.

BLUEBALL
(UK) Morris Goldstein, an associate of Jack Spot. One testicle was reputed to be blue. As a euphemism he was also known as Blueboy.

BOO-HOO
Max Hoff; Philadelphian gangster of the 1920s.

BOTTLES
Ralph Capone, brother of Al, because he worked in a bottling plant.

BROKEN TOOTH KOI
Wan Kuok Koi, 14K Triad leader in Macau, following damage to his mouth in his early days as a streetfighter.

BUGSY
Benjamin Siegel, 'founder' of Las Vegas and shot dead in 1947.

CADILLAC FRANK
Frank Salemne of the Winter Hill mob in Boston.

CALAMITY JANE
Martha Jane Cannary, the outlaw, possibly because she had syphilis.

CATTLE KATE
(US 19c) Ella Watson, prostitute who took to cattle rustling and was hanged.

CHOPPER
Mark Read, the Australia hard-man, named after the self-mutilation of his ears.

CRAZY HORSE
Ass. Comm. David Powis.

DAVE COURTNEONI
Dave Courtney.

DODGER
Jack Mullins, East End enforcer from the 1920s to his death in the 1970s.

DUTCH SCHULTZ
Arthur Flegenheimer. The name was taken as a tribute to the leader of the earlier gang from Frog Hollow, New York.

EL ALACRAN
(Mexican) Henry Loaiza Ceballos, The Scorpion. Alleged to have planned the chainsaw massacre of 107 peasants in Valle de Cauca.

FAT BOY
Arthur Thompson jnr., shot outside his Glasgow home in 1991, son of the legendary Glasgow gang leader.

FIVE DAY JOHNNY
(UK 1960s) John DuRose, London police officer known for the speed with which he solved murder cases.

FLIP FLOP
Clyde Smaldone of the Denver Crime Family, because of a withered hand.

GOLF BAG
Sam Hunt, a Capone associate who carried his machine gun in a golf bag.

GREAZY THUMB
(Chicago) Jake Guzik, pimp and racketeer who originally worked in a café.

HOOTER
Ernie Millen, Commander of the Flying Squad, from the size of his nose.

ICE PICK WILLIE
Israel Alderman, from his use of that weapon.

ITALIAN ALBERT
Albert Dimes, Billy Hill's right-hand man.

ITALIAN JOCK
Victor Dimes, Albert Dimes' brother.

JACK SPOT
Jack Comer or Camacho, the London gangleader of the 1950s because, he said, if anyone was in a spot they called for him or, said others, because he had an unattractive mole.

JACKIE THE LACKEY
Jacky Cerone, originally a chauffeur before becoming a Chicago Don.

JIMMY THE PLEASER
(UK 1960s) James Lawley, because of his sexual prowess.

KID DROPPER
Nathan Kaplan, labour racketeer,

from his skill with the dropped wallet confidence trick.

LEGS
Jack Diamond, acquired either through his ability to outrun the police in his youth or his prowess on the dance floor.

LITTLE AUGIE
Anthony Carfano, one of the last big time pre-syndicate Jewish gangsters. In 1927 when he was killed his garment industry rackets were handed over to Louis Lepke.

LITTLE CAESAR
Philly Jacobs, reputed leader of the East End Dixon gang of the early 1970s.

LITTLE LEGS
(UK 1990s) John Lloyd, because of deformities.

LORD OF THE SKIES
Amado Carillo Fuentes Colombian drug dealer with a penchant for owning Boeing 727s.

LUCKY
Charles Luciano, because he had survived a one-way ride. Imprisoned in 1936 for controlling prostitutes and deported from the

United States to Italy, he died in 1962.

MA

Kate Barker, mother of the Barker boys. Killed in a shoot-out in 1935. Either she was 'a dumpy old woman' or, according to J. Edgar Hoover, 'a veritable beast of prey' and the brains behind the Barker-Karpis gang.

MACHINE GUN

Jack McGurn, planner of the St Valentine's Day Massacre.
George R. Kelly, one time Public Enemy No 1. He died in 1954 in prison serving a sentence for kidnapping.

MAD

Frank Fraser, a member of the Richardson Gang in the so-called Torture Trial of 1966. Committed to three mental hospitals.

MAD AXEMAN

Frank Mitchell, killed on the orders of the Krays who had organised his escape from Dartmoor.

MAD DOG

Vincent Coll, named after he shot a child in an attack on several members of the Schultz organi-

sation in July 1923. He was acquitted but later killed as he made a telephone call.

MARM

Fredericka Mandelbaum, the most powerful of the New York receivers of the 1880s.

MESSY MARVIN

Ronald Moran. In 1997 he became a supergrass after his arrest for being involved in a shoot-out with a Colombo crime figure. He was known in his milieu as Messy Marvin, a name dating back to his untidiness as a child. He later gave evidence against his mother.

MILWAUKEE PHIL

Chicago-based Felix Alderisio, from his control of prostitution in that city.

MR BIG

Arnold Rothstein, the man who fixed the 1919 World Series.

MR NEIL

Aniello Dellacroce, underboss of the Gambino crime family, from his businesslike appearance.

MR RENT-A-KILL

Chris Flannery, Australian contract killer who disappeared

in mysterious circumstances on 9 May 1985.

NAILS
Samuel J. Morton, because he was tough as nails and had a fine World War One record. A Chicago killer he died in a riding accident. The offending horse was killed by a number of gangsters including Bugs Moran.

NIPPER
(UK 1960s) Leonard Read, because of his size, the man who investigated the Krays.

OLD SHAKESPEARE
(US 1890s) Carrie Brown, New York prostitute known for her ability to quote from the plays. She was murdered in her room in circumstances which led to somewhat fanciful suggestions that she might be a victim of Jack the Ripper.

PAPILLON
French criminal, Henri Charrière, either from a tattoo or his penchant for bow ties (*papillons in French*).

PILLOW
Carmelo Fresina, St Louis gangster shot in the buttocks who then carried a pillow with him.

PRETTY
Louis Amberg, a New York contract killer, because of his extreme ugliness.

PRETTY BOY
James Arthur Floyd, because of his extreme good looks.

PUBLIC ENEMY NO. ONE
John Dillinger, Alvin 'Creepy' Karvin and many others. J. Edgar Hoover compiled a list of the most wanted criminals and it became something of a privilege to reach the status of the list.

RAT
(1920s) Confidence trickster Dapper Dan Collins, from the initials of his real name, Robert Arthur Tourbillon.

RED MAX
Emil Allard, 1930s pimp killed in Soho.

RICHIE THE BOOT
Ruggiero Boiardo, from his bootlegging connections.

ROSE MAN OF SING SING
Charles E. Chapin, New York newspaper editor who killed his wife and spent the remainder of his life developing the rose garden at that prison.

RUBY
Jack Sparkes, because as a young man, having stolen a maharajah's rubies, he gave them away thinking they were worthless.

SCARFACE
Al Capone. It referred to a slash given him by Frank Gallucio whilst he was working in/annoying patrons of Frankie Yale's bar cum brothel in the Bronx. Capone had been molesting a girl. In later years he would falsely say it had been acquired during overseas service with the so-called Lost Battalion in the First World War.

SCARFACE JOCK
Victor Russo, Billy Hill admirer who allowed himself to be slashed and then falsely blamed Hill's rival, Jack Spot.

SCOTCH JACK
Jack Buggy, Glasgow-born Soho enforcer killed in the Mount Street Bridge Club in May 1967.

SLIPPERS
(1930s) Louis Brindisi, Denver bootlegger who could not wear shoes after his feet suffered frostbite in an attack on a rival's warehouse.

TATERS
George Chatham, the London burglar because of his continual complaint about the cold following his imprisonment in Dartmoor.

TEETS
Sam Battaglia, Chicago gangster, because of the muscularity of his chest.

THE BOBBED HAIRED BANDIT
(1920-30s) Lilian Goldstein, getaway driver for Ruby Sparkes, from her then fashionable hairstyle.

THE CAMEL
(1930s) Murray Humphreys, New York crime figure, because of his penchant for camel hair coats.

THE CAPTAIN
Ronnie Bender, a Kray associate.

THE CHIN
Vincente Gigante, Genovese Don.

THE COLONEL
Ronnie Kray, George Robinson from the Brink's Mat Robbery. George Copley, from South London, and many others.

THE GENERAL
(1980s-1990s) Martin Cahill, the Irish crime figure killed by the IRA.

THE GENTLE DON
Angelo Bruno, head of the Philadelphia Mafia, killed in 1980, an associate of Albert Dimes the second in command of Billy Hill.

THE HAT
Jack McVitie, because of his unwillingness to reveal his baldness. Killed by Reggie Kray.

THE HUMAN FLY
(1920s) George W. McGrath, the Scots burglar and other housebreakers because of their ability to climb the outside of buildings.

THE LICENSEE
Thomas McGraw, Glasgow hardman because of his interests in public houses. Acquitted of a substantial drug conspiracy in 1998.

THE MAGPIE
Tony Maffia, because of his acquisitive habits, receiver and friend of prison escaper Alfie Hinds. Killed in May 1968.

THE MARSEILLES TIGRESS
Stephanie St Claire, a 1920s Harlem Numbers Runner who clashed with Dutch Schultz and survived.

THE OVERLORD
(1960s-1990s) James Anderson, a Sydney colourful racing identity.

THE RAM
Joe Salardino because of his tendency to grab his opponents by their ears and headbutt them. In later life as he became forgetful he would fail to remove his spectacles before the operation.

THE RIFLEMAN
Stephen Flemmi, Boston associate of James Whitey Bulger.

THE TWINS
Ronnie and Reggie Kray.

THE WAREHOUSEMAN
John Gilligan. Dublin criminal, because of his speciality in breaking into warehouses.

THE WEASEL
Jimmy Frattanno, because of his ability to weasel himself out of a difficult situation. He was one of the first leading members of the Mafia to become a Federal witness.

THREE-FINGER BROWN
Thomas Lucchese, from the loss of a finger in an accident and named after a baseball player who had suffered a similar injury.

TITANIC THOMPSON
Alvin Clarence Thomas, gambler and conman, from his escape from the ship. He was a member of the poker game in which Arnold Rothstein played before he was murdered.

TONY DUCKS
Anthony Corallo, from his ability to duck convictions until 1986 when he was sentenced to 100 years.

TOUGH TONY
Tony Anastasio, New York docks racketeer, brother of Albert Anastasia who had changed the last letter of his name to spare his mother adverse publicity.

TRIGGER MIKE
(1950s) Michael Coppola, Florida hitman known for his ferocity and short temper.

TURKISH ABBI
Ahmet Abdullah, South London crime figure shot in a betting shop. Two men were charged and acquitted.

UNCLE FRANK
Frank Costello, long-time leader of the New York Mafia.

WAXEY GORDON
Irving Wexler, master fixer and associate of Arnold Rothstein.

WIZARD OF ODDS
Donald Angelini and Otto Abandano, because of their mathematical ability and talent in fixing the numbers game.

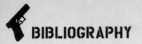

BIBLIOGRAPHY

Beale, P., (ed) **A CONCISE DICTIONARY OF SLANG AND UNCONVENTIONAL ENGLISH** (1989) London, Routledge.

Bentley, W.K. and Corbett, J.M., **PRISON SLANG** (1992) Jefferson, North Carolina, McFarland.

Chapman, R.L., **AMERICAN SLANG** (1987) New York, Harper & Row.

De Sola, R., **CRIME DICTIONARY** (1988) New York, Facts on File Publications.

Devlin, A., **PRISON PATTER** (1996) Winchester, Waterside Press.

Fabian, R., **FABIAN OF THE YARD** (1955) London, Heirloom Modern World Library. — **THE ANATOMY OF CRIME** (1970) London, Pelham Books.

Green, J., **THE DICTIONARY OF CONTEMPORARY SLANG** (1984) London, Pan Books. —**THE SLANG THESAURUS** (1988) Harmondsworth, Penguin Books.

Hornadge, B., **AUSTRALIAN SLANGUAGE** (1989) Port Melbourne, Mandarin.

Maurer, D.W., **LANGUAGE OF THE UNDERWORLD** (1981) Kentucky, Univ of Kentucky Press.

Major, C.., **THE DICTIONARY OF AFRO-AMERICAN SLANG** (1970) New York, International.

McDonald, J., **A DICTIONARY OF OBSCENITY, TABOO AND EUPHEMISM** (1988) London, Sphere Books.

Mezzrow, M., **REALLY THE BLUES** (1946) New York, Random House.

Milner, C. and R., **BLACK PLAYERS** (1973) London, Michael Joseph.

Morton, J., **LOWSPEAK** (1989) London, Angus & Robertson.

GANGSTER SPEAK: A DICTIONARY OF CRIMINAL AND SEXUAL SLANG

Partridge, E., **A DICTIONARY OF THE UNDERWORLD** (1961) London, Routledge & Keegan Paul. —**THE PENGUIN DICTIONARY OF SLANG** (1986) Harmondsworth, Penguin.

Patrick, J., **A GLASGOW GANG OBSERVED** (1973) London, Eyre Methuen.

Scarne, J., **SCARNE'S COMPLETE GUIDE TO GAMBLING** (1961) New York, Simon & Schuster.

Simes, G., **A DICTIONARY OF AUSTRALIAN UNDERWORLD SLANG** (1993) Melbourne, Oxford University Press.

Powis, D., **THE SIGNS OF CRIME** (1977) London, McGraw Hill.

Stroud, C., **CLOSE PURSUIT** (1988) Markham, Ont., Penguin Books.

Tempest, P., **LAG'S LEXICON** (1950) London, Routledge & Keegan Paul.

Wentworth, H. and Flexner, S.B., **DICTIONARY OF AMERICAN SLANG** (1960) London, George G. Harrap.